D1146896

FAVOURITE PLACES IN
BRITTANY

TEXT
PATRICK HUCHET

PHOTOS
YVON BOËLLE

TRANSLATION: ENTREPRISES 35

Éditions   Ouest-France

LA MANCHE

CÔTE DE GRANITE ROSE

CÔTE DU GOËLO

AU PAYS DES GOÉMONIERS

Pointe du Château

Sept-Îles

Loguivy-de-la-Mer

Île de Bréhat

Plougrescant

Ploubazlanec
Paimpol

Perros-Guirec

Tréguier

Plouezec

Île de Batz

Pointe de Bloscon

Saint-Pol-de-Léon

Lanmeur

Lannion

Abbaye de Beauport

Port de Gwin Zegal

Plouha

DES LÉGENDES

Phare de l'Île Vierge

Illiz Coz

Lilia
Plouguerneau

Vallon du Traon

Lannilis

Le Folgoët

Morlaix

Guingamp

Baie de Saint-Brie

CÔTE

LES ABERS

Aber Wrac'h

Pont-Krac'h

ENCLOS PAROISSIAUX

Landivisiau

Saint-Thégonnec
Guimiliau

Châtelaudren

Île d'Ouessant

Île de Molène

Pointe de Corsen

Landerneau

Lampaul-Guimiliau

MONTS D'ARRÉE

FORÊT D'HUELGOAT

Plougastel-Daoulas

La Martyre

Elorn

Brest

Île de Béniguet

Sizun

Commana

Roc'h
Trévézel
384

Saint-Rivoal

Brennilis

Saint-Brieuc

Lam

Pointe St-Mathieu

Notre-Dame de Rocamadour
Camaret-sur-Mer
Alignements de Lagatjar

Presqu'île de Crozon

Rade de Brest

Huelgoat

Marais du Yeun Elez

Carhaix-Plouguer

Rostrenen

Gouarec

Mont Me

Langast

CAMARET-SUR-MER

Pointe de Pen-Hir

Brasparts

Plovenez-du-Faou

LANDES DU MÉ

Crozon

Menez Hom
330

Pleyben

Canal de Nantes à Brest

297

Cap de la Chèvre

Baie de Douarnenez

Châteaulin

Aube

Loudéac

MONTAGNES NOIRES

Pointe du Raz

Locronan

Douarnenez

Odé

FINISTÈRE

Île de Sein

Plozévet

Pouldreuzic

Quimper

Vallée du Blavet

Pontivy

Baie

Plonéour-Lanvern

PAYS BIGOUDEN

Bieuzy

Saint-Nicodème
Pluméliau

d'Audierne

Pont-l'Abbé

Sainte-Marine

Concarneau

Saint-Nicolas-des-Eaux

Quistinic

Joss

Saint-Jean-Trolimon

Île Tudy

Quimperlé

Poul Fetan

LA VALLÉE DU BLAVET

Notre-Dame de Tronoën
Notre-Dame de la Joie

Loctudy
Lesconil

Pont-Aven

Blavet

MORBIHAN

Pointe de Penmarc'h

Penmarc'h
Guilvinec

Pointe de Trévignon

Hennebont

LANDES L

Îles de Glénan

Lorient

Locoal-Mendon

Brec'h

Vannes

OCÉAN ATLANTIQUE

Île de Groix

PAYS D'AURAY

Auray

Île de Gavrinis

Île aux Mo

Ploemel

Larmor-Baden

Île d'

La Trinité-sur-Mer
Carnac

Séné

Locmariaquer

Port Navalo

Arzon

Saint-Arme

Golfe du Morbihan

Sarzeau

Presqu'île de Quiberon

Quiberon

Saint-Gildas-de-Rhuys

GOLFE DU MORBIHAN

Pointe du Conguel

Île de Houat

Belle-Île

Île de Hoëdic

Pointe du Croisic

CÔTE

LE DÉCOR PEINT D'ÉGLISES COSTARMORICAINES

CONTENTS

0   25   50 km

GOLFE DE SAINT-MALO

CÔTE D'ÉMERAUDE

MANCHE

Cap Fréhel
Saint-Lunaire
Saint-Malo
Dinard
Cancale
Pointe du Grouin
Baie du Mont-Saint-Michel
-st-le-Guildo
Saint-Briac-sur-Mer
Dol-de-Bretagne

DINAN ET
LES RIVES DE
LA RANCE

Rance
Canal d'Ille-et-Rance

Dinan
Combourg
Fougères

CÔTES-
ARMOR
Rance

St-Méen-le-Grand

ILLE-ET-VILAINE

Cesson-Sévigné

MARCHES

MAYENNE

Mauron
Concoret
Tréhorenteuc
Paimpont
sans
tour
256
FORÊT DE
BROCÉLIANDE
Campénéac
Ploërmel

Rennes

Vitré
Châteaubourg

DE

BRETAGNE

Vilaine

La Gacilly

La Guerche-de-Bretagne

Nantes à Brest

Redon
Marais de Redon
Fégréac

Châteaubriant

CANAL DE
NANTES À BREST

PARC NATUREL
RÉGIONAL
DE BRIÈRE
Blain

Canal de Nantes à Brest

L'Erdre

Herbignac
La Chapelle-des-Marais
Saint-Lyphard
Île de Fédrun
Bréca
Saint-Malo-de-Guersac
Saint-André-des-Eaux

Quiheix

Sucé-sur-Erdre

Loire

Saint-Nazaire

MAINE-ET-LOIRE

PAYS DE
RETZ

Nantes

AMOUR
Île de
Noirmoutier

LOIRE-
ATLANTIQUE

Clisson
CLISSON

VENDÉE

BRITTANY...

with passion

I was born in the village of Branhoc, in the commune of Locoal-Mendon, a delightful spot tucked away among pastures on the banks of the Étel ria (Morbihan), the exact reflection of the double facets of our fine land, "between turf and surf".

My childhood here was happy and joyful, with its rhythm of school and, above all... holidays. These were times for walks along the small country paths, bathing at the "big beach" of Locoal, and listening there to Claude, a poor man who had taken refuge in a little hut nearby, and who played his accordion for us.

Of course, these melodies had nothing, simply nothing, to do with the original score but, nonetheless, we were happy, and Claude was the first to roar with laughter about these massacred songs. Happiness can be so simple, among friends! Close to this famous "big beach" (which some dared mention had rather "sticky" silt), there was a lane bordered with hundred-year old oak trees, which led to a thicket abandoned to the heath and the brambles: "Cadoudal lane". Miraculously, it was preserved from the ravages of the re-allocation of land in the sixties, and this path with wide vistas over the sea preserved the memory of the most illustrious of Chouans (Royalists after the Revolution), Georges Cadoudal... and at the very end of the path one of the finest views opens up over the Étel ria.

Each summer, I take a real pleasure in unveiling these hidden treasures to amazed tourists, astonished that they had never imagined the existence of such a natural heritage, hardly mentioned except for a few lines lost in most guidebooks.

I have described the land of my birth at length since it is in the image of the whole of Brittany: so dense and varied that it would be

The Étel ria, between turf and surf.

impossible to describe its special character in only a few pages... So now let's set off to discover it...

Is Brittany conceivable without the megaliths of Carnac?

Without Raz Point, is it imaginable?

Taking the risk of appearing pompous, I dare answer yes: yes, there is another Brittany, discreet, secret, that of the perfumed paths climbing up the face of the Goëlo cliffs or winding down to the deepest of the Brière marshes.

A Brittany which is dynamic, a Brittany which is mystical, which manifests itself in the stone and the Kersanton granite of the Parish closes.

And then there are all these legends which flourish in the woods and heaths, in the forest of Brocéliande, and in this giant chaos of rocks rolling down Huelgoat...

"Brittany is a universe", sang the poet Saint-Pol Roux, falling under the charm of Camaret. Nothing is nearer the truth, seeing the endless books and magazines enthusiastically describing either its "extraordinary heritage" or its "fabulous landscapes".

However, our aim here is much more modest, to make you share our favourite places, strolling along the paths crossing this land, whose deepest identity was so well described by Julien Gracq:

"For the chosen few, visiting Brittany is not what counts. What counts is to leave it wishing to stay and live there, the ear glued against this deep murmuring shell.

And its appeal is that of a cloister whose wall has a breach open to the high seas: the sea, the wind, the sky, the bare earth, and nothing.

This is the realm of the soul."

DEGEMER MAT E BREIZH!

WELCOME TO BRITTANY!

Patrick Huchet

*The "Crux Prostlon",
the Prostlon Cross, a very
beautiful Gallic stela, just
outside the little town of
Locoal.*

Ille-et-Vilaine

between history and legend

THE BORDERLANDS OF BRITTANY: LA GUERCHE-DE-BRETAGNE, VITRÉ, FOUGÈRES

Brittany was ravaged by the Norman hordes in the 9th and 10th centuries, and then was reunited under the glorious victor over the Norsemen, Alain Barbe-Torte. After taking Nantes back from them in 937, he finally drove them out of the Duchy in 939.

The Dukes of Brittany built up a powerful defensive system on the "frontier", the Borderlands, to assert their power against the pretensions of the Anglo-Norman Plantagenets (12th century) and then the kings of France. This was the role given to the strongholds of Pontorson, Saint-James, Craon, Segré, Montaigu, on the French side, and Fougères, Vitré, Ancenis, Clisson, Machecoul, on the Breton side.

Out of the nine Breton Baronies of the Middle Ages, the three we are going to visit have kept a definite medieval character: La Guerche-de-Bretagne, Vitré, Fougères.

*Left: **The Valley of no Return in Brocéliande**.*

Vitré and its castle at dusk.

lord, Menguen, received his fiefdom from the hands of Geoffroy I Duke of Brittany (who died in 1008). He was followed by thirty-seven others, the best known without any doubt being Bertrand du Guesclin who bought La Guerche in 1379.

As a mark of honour, the lords of La Guerche shared, with those of Vitré, Châteaugiron and Aubigné the privilege of carrying the Bishop of Rennes' chair the day he entered his cathedral.

La Guerche castle, originally a simple

The collegiate church of Guerche-de-Bretagne. The altar of the North side aisle has a big wooden statue of the Virgin (17th century) which has been worshipped from long ago... and these days too, as can be seen from the many requests for intercession, written by the faithful, in the book left for this purpose in the church.

La Guerche-de-Bretagne

This little city, fortified in times gone by, grew around its castle and its well known collegiate church between the 10th and 12th centuries. Around the year one thousand, its first over-

In the fifth bay of the collegiate church, a stained glass window from 1536 represents the Bishop of Rennes, Yves Mahyeuc, kneeling next to the Virgin. His patron saint is behind him, dressed in a long red robe with an ermine waistcoat. At his feet, two little angels hold up the episcopal escutcheon.

wooden keep, gave way to a grand stone building in the 15th century, which unfortunately was destroyed in 1739. Although the "castel" may have disappeared, the small city nonetheless preserved its medieval character with its elegant wood-framed houses especially in the central square. Each Tuesday, a market is held on this vast esplanade (and the narrow streets around), one of the oldest markets of France; it has been mentioned since...the year of grace 1121!

Recumbent figure and tomb of Guillaume II, founder of the collegiate church.

After admiring the fine wood framed houses with their half timbering (16th-17th centuries), which are evidence of past prosperity, you will come to the Notre-Dame Basilica whose origin dates back to the 13th century. In fact, in 1206 Guillaume II, the ninth lord of La Guerche, founded a collegiate church with twelve canons "*to save his soul and those of his forebears and descendants*". In the choir of this church, raised to the rank of minor basilica in 1951, you can see his tomb (he died on September 4th, 1223).

There are some magnificent stalls in the choir, all in sculpted wood: the arm-rests, the tilt-up misericords and the end uprights are covered with elegant foliage and figures full of originality. On the south side, the misericords represent various scenes of paradise on earth, the creation of Adam and Eve... On the north side, the seven capital sins are represented in very picturesque scenes: *the jealous who wants to grab the moon between his teeth, the proud who want to fill the universe with the sound of their exploits, a drunkard still drinking from his barrel while others are trying to lift him up...*

The stained glass windows are also noteworthy: in the second bay from the entrance, seven panels of primitive glass windows depicting the tree of Jesse are preserved. The third bay possesses a stained glass window representing the last judgement; it dates from 1537.

Vitré

I love to lose myself in the maze of narrow streets of the small medieval cities of Brittany: Auray, Josselin, Quimperlé, Quimper... In Vitré, I was in bliss!

The castle

Once again it stands in a strategic position, a promontory perfect for building a stronghold, which is the origin of the first "castel" to be built on a schist spur dominating the river Vilaine. We know little about the buildings erected by the first lords of Vitré; Riwallon (one of the knights of Geoffroy I, Duke of Brittany), and then Robert I, one of his sons.

The simple keep dating from the year one thousand made way, in the 13th century, to a strong fortress, the work of André III, Baron of Vitré. Vitré was the seat of one of the nine baronies of the Duchy of Brittany and played a major role on these famous Borderlands, the line of defence between Brittany and France.

This was also the aim of the walls built between 1220 and 1240, around the present old town. These ramparts are still visible to the south (thus the "Bridole

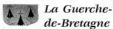

La Guerche-de-Bretagne

WHERE TO FIND INFORMATION?
Tourist office of the Guerche region
Place Charles-de-Gaulle
35130 La Guerche-de-Bretagne
Tel. : 02 99 96 30 78 —
Fax : 02 99 96 15 06
Website:
http ://www. region-bretagne. fr

Top left: **Detail of the choir stalls, Renaissance decor.**

The Saint-Laurent tower.

The main entrance to the majestic castle, built between the 11th and 13th centuries by the barons of Vitré.

The merchants of Vitré

The prosperity of the town, which can be seen from its picturesque houses, is greatly due to the trade it developed between the 15th and 18th centuries, that of canvas, heavy material used especially for making sails.

In 1472, forty-three Vitré merchants founded the Overseas Merchants Brotherhood, selling their wares in particular to Northern Europe, England, Spain, Portugal... and as far as South America! The decline is explained by the repeal of the Edict of Nantes by Louis XIV, in 1685. The merchants, who were mainly Protestants, took exile in more clement skies, such as Holland and England.

in Vitré, with its gabled houses, decorated in Renaissance style, with pilasters, ornamented façades... which made the writer Pol de Courcy say *"they seemed to be like good neighbours, leaning one against the other, like whispering scandalmongers".*

Number 12 of rue Saint-Louis was occupied by the first Protestant temple of the town; the Brittany parliament held its meetings there several times.

The wood framed houses of the Embas, Four, and Poterie streets, some with porches and pointed roofs, constitute an attractive medieval "Landscape", full of bars and restaurants, and terraces where it is pleasant to spend summer evenings.

Walks in and around Vitré

Apart from the walled town, Vitré has many other suggestions for walks:

"The Tertres Noirs Path". *Take the Rachapt road (in the district of the same name), then climb the 300 m leading you to a superb panorama over the castle, the old town and the valley.*

The Botanical Garden. *Previously, this was the park of the Marie castle, the residence of the lords of Vitré from the 17th century.*

The Rochers-Sévigné château. *About 5 km from Vitré, this elegant dwelling is haunted by the memory of the famous Madame de Sévigné... whose fine full-length portrait is on display in one of the wings. From here, she wrote her famous "Letters", which have passed into literary posterity.*

Embas street.

Tower" next to the Post Office) and along the "Val promenade" (access through the grill gate located behind the Post Office).

The old walled town

Apart from the castle and the Notre-Dame church (15th-16th centuries), its attraction also lies above all in its cobbled streets, bordered by half-timbered houses, all askew.

The rue de la Baudrerie owes its name to the *baudroyeurs*, the leather craftsmen and workers who lived there. This is the best preserved road

 Vitré

WHERE TO FIND INFORMATION?
Tourist office
Place Saint-Yves 35500 Vitré
Tel.: 02 99 75 04 46 —
Fax: 02 99 74 02 01
E-mail: vitre@mail35-galeode.fr

Fougères

« At this moment I am in fougères (ferns) country, in a town which has an ancient castle flanked by old towers, the most splendid in the world, with water-mills, running streams, rocks, gardens full of roses... »

One evening in June 1836, Victor Hugo had this vision of the medieval city, from the belvedere of the public garden ... How could Fougères dream of more illustrious advertising! The great writer described in these few chosen words the main attractions of the town.

The castle

Just like many of the medieval cities, Fougères was born at the dawn of the year one thousand, on a promontory dominating the Nançon marshes and river. The original simple keep gave way to a castle, constantly strengthened by the lords of Fougères.

Raoul II (1130-1194), one of the best known barons, tried to resist Henry II Plantagenet, king of England, but after the siege of 1166, the castle was taken and demolished. Raoul II rebuilt it to make a powerful fortress. In the 13th century, Jeanne de Fougères added to the defensive system (in particular with the Mélusine and Gobelin towers) and surrounded the town with high walls.

Saint-Sulpice, a quarter with a medieval atmosphere

In the 11th century, the population settled around the foot of the castle and the first artisan activities were developed: tanning, tinting, cloth manufacturing... due to the proximity of the river Nançon.

From the 14th to 16th century, Fougères had the monopoly of the production of red cloth; "cardinals' scarlet". You will find this Middle Ages atmosphere on Marchix Square (with its wood framed houses from the 17th century), in Tanneur (tanning) street, Filature (weaving) lane, etc.

With its key position on the Borderlands of the Duchy of Brittany, the castle of Fougères was further strengthened by two towers ("La Tourasse" and "La Françoise") in the 15th century, to face the progress in artillery. This castle, rightly considered as one of the most important medieval fortresses in Europe, is a real "book" of the history of military architecture. A visit not to be missed.

Saint-Sulpice church. Detail from a stained glass window representing the fairy Mélusine.

Saint-Sulpice church. The coat of arms of the Duke of Brittany. Detail from the north medieval altarpiece.

"Fougères in full letters", an "in situ" literary circuit

What a splendid idea, to discover the texts of the great writers (Balzac, Chateaubriand, Hugo, Guéhenno, Gracq...) on the very spots which inspired them. From Aristide-Briand square up to Pinterie street, following the National road, the public garden, the Duchesse-Anne stairway, etc. Twenty-six plates and easels provide a most pleasant literary promenade.

The Fougères ramparts seen from the public gardens.

Right: Marchix Square. Old houses in the Saint-Sulpice district.

 Fougères

WHERE TO FIND INFORMATION?
Tourist office
1, place Aristide-Briand
35300 Fougères
Tourist information
Tel.: 02 99 94 12 20 —
Fax: 02 99 94 77 30
Open all year round
Welcome to Fougères country
Tel.: 02 99 94 60 30 —
Fax: 02 99 94 30 39

The Saint-Sulpice church should not be neglected. It is a fine example of flamboyant Gothic, and has two superb granite altar pieces, 16th century stained glass windows and a statue of Notre-Dame-des-Marais, which according to tradition already stood in the 12th century castle. The statue was victim of the pillage by the English in 1166, but was "miraculously" found in the moats, in the 14th century.

Take Pinterie street (where they produced pewter pints) which links the Saint-Sulpice district to the "upper town" and continue your stroll, discovering other monuments.

Saint-Briac. The Emerald Balcony.

THE JEWELS OF THE EMERALD COAST, FROM SAINT-BRIAC TO CANCALE

"We all owe something to Brittany. It illuminated our youth, gave us many poetic emotions, and reanimated our love for Art..."

Émile Bernard paid this homage, so beautiful, in his Mémoires to Saint-Briac and the Emerald Coast, the source of inspiration for many artists: in the summer of 1902, Debussy composed his major work here, "the Sea"; and several years later Picasso took his inspiration from a beach scene at Dinard, to paint his famous work: "Women playing with a ball"...

From the heaths of Cape Fréhel to the marine expanses of Mont-Saint-Michel, the sea shines with an incomparable colour: emerald... Boarding now...

Saint-Briac-sur-Mer

This peaceful seaside resort, the cradle of many high seas captains has managed to preserve its very fine stone houses, one against the other in the narrow streets surrounding the Parish church.

Following Petit-Port street, you will reach the "Emerald Balcony", a vast esplanade overlooking the ocean. Here, a hundred years ago, there were wheat fields, painted wonderfully, in 1891, by the artist Émile Bernard, in his "harvest at the sea-side" (to be seen at the Orsay Museum in Paris). And then stone took over from the ears of wheat... it happens like that... but it is not all negative these days:

Between Saint-Briac and Saint-Lunaire, there are several creeks for those who wish to idle between golden sand and emerald sea.

 Saint-Briac-sur-Mer

WHERE TO FIND INFORMATION?
Tourist office
La Houle 35800 Saint-Briac-sur-Mer
Tel.: 02 99 88 32 47

The Grand Hotel, transformed into flats these days.

In addition, the Old Town shelters one of the rare Romanesque churches in Brittany, and we shall begin our visit of this charming locality here.

The old church

It stands on Pillory Place (where, in the Middle Ages, the condemned were attached and exhibited to the public) and there is no way of guessing what "treasures" are to be found by entering: the Romanesque nave (early 11th century), with three bays, and six semicircular arches; the recumbent figures of the lords of Pontual and Pontbriand and the tomb of Saint Lunaire.

In fact, the latter is a Gallo-Roman sarcophagus covered, in the 16th century, by a granite slab which is sculpted, in relief, with a statue of Saint Lunaire clothed in his episcopal vestments. Note, on the right side of his chest, a dove with open wings, holding a "movable altar" in its beak, a reminder of the legend according to which two gracious doves brought this indispensable altar to the saint, to carry out his mission, which his fellow travellers had thrown into the sea, to

the customs officers' path, in particular, is a very pleasant walk along the edge of the coast, from Béchet beach to Garde-Guérin Point, passing by the superb "balconies" of the Essarts and La Haye Point.

Detail of a recumbent figure in the old Saint-Lunaire church.

Décollé Point. Sunrise over Saint-Malo bay.

Saint-Lunaire

Between land and sea, sailors and peasants, life passed peacefully in Saint-Lunaire until, at the end of the 19th century, a rich banker built the Grand Hotel, facing the main beach. Without waiting for the renown of its close and famous neighbour, Dinard, the resort of Saint-Lunaire was born, surrounded by superb villas from the "Belle Époque", which we still admire today.

try to lighten their ship caught in a terrible storm.

Walks and rambling

Apart from the customs officers' path which faithfully follows the coastline, the tourist office suggests three loops: "Saint-Lunaire, Breton village", "Country and Coast walk", and "Saint-Lunaire Sea Resort".

A walk is a good way to discover the "special" little corners of the Amitié

 Saint-Lunaire

MORE INFORMATION?
Tourist office
Boulevard du Général-de-Gaulle 35800 Saint-Lunaire
Tel./Fax: 02 99 46 31 09

valley, the superb "Belle Epoque" villas along the Rochers Boulevard, and the best panorama over the bay of Saint-Malo, from Décollé Point.

Dinard

Hidden from all earthly regard, in the "Goule aux Fées" grotto (Fairies' Throat) near Saint-Enogat beach, elegant ladies gifted with supernatural powers carefully watched over the cradle of a little hamlet: Saint-Enogat.

After a deep sleep of more than... a thousand years, families originating from England came to awaken the sleeping village: an English consul was installed in the Priory in 1836, soon followed by other consuls and members of high society. In 1857, the Fabers built the Sainte-Catherine villa. In 1859, the Dinard hotel was erected (nowadays the Grand Hotel). During the following decades, luxurious hotels grew up like mushrooms, to such a point that at the beginning of 1900, Dinard was given the title of the "resort with a hundred hotels", the most famous in Europe. A century later, it has lost none of its charm... on the contrary, its "Belle Epoque" villas, carefully maintained, have now been classified as historic monuments and are part of the three walks suggested by the tourist office.

Three walks around the villas

The first circuit takes you towards the vast beach, called the Écluse (lock) beach. From the esplanade, you can see a wide range of hotels and villas, such as the Royal Hotel, the Grand Bé villa, the Queen Hortense villa...

In the rue des Cèdres (Cedar Street), you can admire the splendid dwellings built by the English colony: the Grand Chalet and the Vieux Moulin, and the Anglican church built in 1870 by Mr Faber, son of the first British resident in Dinard.

Seaside harvest by Émile Bernard (1868-1941).
Paris, Orsay Museum. © RMN - H. Lewandowski.

"The artists' path along the Emerald Coast"

From the Saint-Briac "Emerald Balcony" with its beaches and Dinard cove, seventeen reproductions of paintings, set in the very place where the artists produced their work, are evidence of the considerable contribution of the Emerald Coast to pictorial art.

This gives a unique possibility of regarding these landscapes which inspired so many talented artists: E. Bernard, A. Nozel, E. Vuillard, H. Rivière, P. Picasso, etc.

Books to read: "Emerald Glimpses". The fruit of ten years of devoted research, this exceptional work (424 pages, 600 illustrations including 200 in colour) is on sale in bookshops or can be obtained from the author-publisher, J.-P. Bihr, 22750 Saint-Jacut-de-la-Mer (tel. 02 96 27 70 32).

One of the "Belle Epoque" villas, which can be glimpsed from the Malouine walk.

The villa Eugénie, the Resort museum

This villa, built in 1867 following the plans of the architect Jean Pichot, looks like a castle with its four turrets, and is named after the empress Eugénie de Montijo, wife of emperor Napoleon III. These illustrious personages had agreed to launch the "1868 summer season" in Dinard when an incident took place which threw everything into doubt: the empress had a little dog, a "lapdog" which she adored - but which her husband detested!

A small beginning, but with important results: after a violent quarrel when the emperor refused to take the dog with them, Eugénie fled alone to Biarritz... depriving Dinard of this visit which it had been looking forward to so much.

These days the Eugénie villa houses collections from the museum of the canton of Dinard... and an astonishing retrospective of bathing costumes and swimsuits, from 1880 to 1950.

Right: **Saint-Malo bay.**
The ferry leaving for England passes Cézembre island.

Opposite: **The vast beach at Dinard in front of the Casino.**

M. Hennessy, the very wealthy cognac producer).

The way back to the museum follows paths dug out of the cliff, revealing the villas of Bric-à-Brac (now the aquarium), Belle Rive etc.

Walking down towards the Arts and Festival Palace, you will pass in front of the La Surprise villa and its superb mosaic, and then the Alba villa, the casino and the former Terrasses hotel.

The second tour leads you to Malouine Point, where the finest villas are to be found. Risking creating a few jealousies, let us pick out a few beauties: the Ker Willy and Kerosar, Cendrillon...

The third walk begins from the museum of the seaside resort and first of all enables you to admire the villas built by the architect Pichot, before heading for Moulinet Point (the La Garde villa, built around 1880 by

 Dinard

MORE INFORMATION?
Tourist office
2, boulevard Féart, BP 140,
35802 Dinard Cedex
Tel.: 02 99 46 94 12 —
Fax: 02 99 88 21 07

Walks and rambles

Dinard combines the elegance of its villas with the romanticism of its walks, in the image of the "Clair de Lune" (Moonlight) walk, which overwhelmed poets and nature lovers.

The "Clair de Lune" walk

This outing, between Prieuré (Priory) Beach and Moulinet Point, offers a delightful stroll between the iodised odours of the ocean and the perfumes of the garden illuminated at nightfall. Between June 15th and September 15th, the path is lit up and different music is broadcast each evening.

The Port-Breton park

This is facing Prieuré Beach, and offers visitors a 60-acre park, with flowers, trees and bushes.

The patrol path, or the customs officer's path

From Port-Blanc Beach to Plissot Beach, this walk reveals wonderful views, from the Malouine, Moulinet, Vicomté and Jument Points.

Saint-Malo

From every direction, Saint-Malo first gives the vision of a granite fortress, protected by strong ramparts, above which the high cathedral steeple can be seen. This privateers city, reputed over the centuries for its spirit of independence, owes its name to a Welsh monk Mac Clow, who became bishop of Alet in the 6th century, the ancient cradle of the town.

In the 12th century, "Saint-Malo de l'Isle" was created and the medieval walls were built, which were strengthened in the 15th century by a castle, the work of the last Dukes of Brittany. Between the 16th and 18th centuries, sailors and...privateers from Saint-Malo sailed the seas: Jacques Cartier discovered Canada (1534); Duguay-Trouin (1673-1736) and Surcouf (1773-1827) attacked the rich vessels of English and Dutch companies, bringing back a fortune to the crown of France. Saint-Malo became the richest town of the realm. These "Messieurs from Saint-Malo" built their own fabulous houses and dwellings, called the "malouinières", a striking symbol of their great success.

In 1944, 80% of the intra-muros was destroyed. It was rebuilt exactly the same (between 1947 and 1952)

Saint-Malo, independent Republic

This malouine town, faithful to its "Fronde" reputation, ("neither French nor Breton"), proclaimed itself an independent "Republic" in 1590, at the time of the Wars of Religion, refusing alliance with Henri IV king of France, Protestant at that time. The "independence" ended four years later, when the latter changed faith.

The privateer city sheltered by its ramparts at dusk. Seen from Malouine Point.

Nave of the Saint-Vincent Cathedral.

The cafés on Chateaubriand Square, the "in" place of Saint-Malo.

Ship-owner's house. Saint-Louis Bastion. Statue of Duguay-Trouin.

stone by stone, thanks to the joint efforts of the mayor Guy La Chambre and the Historic Monuments.

Saint-Malo intra-muros

Before losing yourself in the narrow streets, to admire the sumptuous stone dwellings, I must recommend that you admire the "Duchess Anne Château" (now the town hall), dominated by its Great Keep (built by Jean V, Duke of Brittany), and then follow the inevitable walk along the ramparts.

After this walk, greatly appreciated by the Malouins - and tourists - you will understand why, since the Middle Ages, Saint-Malo has had the reputation of being a "sea fortress", which the English tried to take many times... but unsuccessfully!

Saint-Vincent cathedral (12th to 18th century)

The nave and the remains of the restored cloister still keep the 12th century Romanesque style. In the middle of the 16th century, the very fine Gothic chancel was built with its anglo-norman flat apse. The contemporary stained glass windows by Max Ingrand and Jean Le Moal diffuse a beautiful light.

As a suggestion, after several experiences, try a walk in Saint-Malo in January; warmth in the middle of winter.

Saint-Malo

MORE INFORMATION?
Tourist office
Port des yachts
35400 Saint-Malo
Tel.: 02 99 56 64 48 —
Fax: 02 99 56 67 00
E-mail: office. de. tourisme.
saint-malo@wanadoo. fr
Website: www. ville-saint-
malo. fr and
www. bretagne-4villes. com

*The marina. Departure
point for the "Route
du Rhum".*

Saint-Malo extra-muros

There is no lack of interesting visits.
Saint-Servan: the city of Alet, the historic cradle of Saint-Malo (remains of the old cathedral); the Solidor tower (the work of Jean IV, Duke of Brittany). It has dominated the estuary of the river Rance since the 14th century and its keep (30 metres high) houses the International Museum of the High Seas Cape-Horners.

The Grand Bé island (facing the intra-muros ramparts) is accessible at low tide. It is the final home of François-René de Chateaubriand (1768-1848), author of "Génie du Christianisme".

There are very pleasant walks, such as that leading from the corniche to the city of Alet, which offers magnificent views over Dinard and the Rance river, and another along the Paramé seafront, as far as Rochebonne Point. Breathe in deeply!

*The "Sillon", a fine walk
between Saint Malo and
Paramé. In the foreground,
tree-trunks acting as break-
waters to protect the dyke.*

L'equipage en péril fait un voeu à N.D. du Verger

Cancale

In 1994 the National Council of culinary arts recognised Cancale as a "notable gourmet site", for the quality of its oysters. This was a fair reward for this town whose tasty shellfish made its fortune: there is no land under the quays of the Houle port... just tons and tons of oyster shells!

The natural riches of the Mont-Saint-Michel bay since the "nights of time" were thought to be inexhaustible (20,000 tons were harvested in 1920), but random harvesting had to be stopped and reserved for dredging at several defined periods: and then the famous "bisquines" (fishing smacks from Cancale) went to sea, all sails in the wind, pulling their drags-nets over the natural oyster fields.

La Houle

The "Houle" (sea surge) is a curious name for a port which is so well protected by a high cliff. On the quay the restaurants and cafés are side by side, offering tempting menus where the oyster is evidently the star. Luckily, Cancale has remained a lively fishing port, proved by the carefully ranged fishing boats along the pier: "Petite Jeanne" (Little Jean), "André-Yann", "Cathy-Laurent", "Steeven-Bastien", etc.

With its iodised odours and gastronomic delights, the "Houle" is also the criss-crossing of little streets behind, between the "Blanche" (sea front) and the cliff. Perhaps you will notice the statuettes of the Virgin Mary on the facades of the fishermens' houses from the 18th and 19th centuries. They are a testimony of a tradition which dates back more than a hundred years: every August 15th the wayside altars along the streets are decorated, and the statuettes are lit up by the flames of candles. And then the chants and canticles resound in honour of the mother of Christ, protector of sailors.

Since oysters have tonic virtues, don't hesitate to eat a few, before attacking the heights and cliffs of the 15 km long coastline.

Trails and paths

From Houle port to Du Guesclin beach, you must go on foot to contemplate fully the magnificent panoramas of the Mont-Saint-Michel Bay, on the one hand, and Saint Malo, on the other. You can take the GR 34 trail (a backpack tour) and loop-tracks, following the routes set out by the Tourist Office.

As you walk, known sites can be seen (Cancale rock, Port-Briac beach, Grouin Point...) and several hidden treasures as well.

The Verger chapel, built around 1870, on the foundations of an earlier building (already venerated by the sailors), holds moving ex-votos (for example, paintings representing boats which escaped shipwreck) and dozens of marble plaques in recognition of the protection received: *"Thank you, Good Mother 1893"*, *"Thank you Mary, for bringing him back on April 7th 1902"*, *"Thank you Little Mother 1979"*...

CAN.87

La Houle port, the ideal place for enjoying oysters... the natural way.

The Daules barracks built in the 18th century on the hill overlooking Daules Point, a solid building in stone and granite, situated just next to the Verger chapel, is evidence of the need to protect the coast at that time from smugglers attempting to land there... as well as armed troops from the "Perfidious Albion"!

Cancale bay was often their target, particularly at the time of the Revolution, and countless Royalist agents landed there.

The customs officers' path and the Verger beach.

Cancale

MORE INFORMATION?
Tourist office
44, rue du Port
35260 Cancale
Tel.: 02 99 89 63 72 —
Fax: 02 99 89 75 08

BROCÉLIANDE,
A LEGENDARY FOREST

*"I looked for the most obscure forest...
the Holy Grail is there, somewhere...
everyone knows... Brittany is haunted by
it. The old people talk about it in the
evenings around the fire. The poets make
marvels out of it. The best, at Arthur's
Court, were possessed by it up to mad-
ness. The Holy Grail has become the
world's dream..."* Julien Gracq.

All lands have their own legends.
Brocéliande is a legend: no path, no
thicket, no clearing without the echo

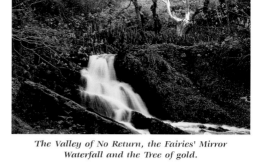

*The Valley of No Return, the Fairies' Mirror
Waterfall and the Tree of gold.*

of King Arthur's cavalries, the fabulous
exploits of the Knights of the Round
Table... Welcome to the kingdom of
magic.

Paimpont

This pleasant market town, set
among trees, retains the memory of
Judicaël, king of Brittany, who founded a monastery here in the 7th century. There are many rare treasures in
the sacristy of the parish church: the
relics of Saint Judicaël, a precious sil-
ver arm reliquary offered to the monks
by the mother of Anne of Brittany, and
a very beautiful Christ in ivory dating
from the 18th century.

Tréhorenteuc church

"The door is within." This inscription,
all in red, above the entrance, leaves a
mystery... which darkens inside, in front
of the mosaics, paintings, stained glass

The legends of the Brocéliande forest

*Their origin lies in the adventures of King
Arthur, his companion Merlin the sorcerer
and the young knight Lancelot of the Lake
(infatuated by Guinevere, King Arthur's
wife). Merlin advised constituting the
Order of the Knights of the Round Table.
The tale of King Arthur relates the (exciting) life of this legendary king, the loves
and achievements of his knights. In the
12th century Chrétien de Troyes made the
"Brécilien" (the name of the forest in the
Middle Ages) the base of their exploits, in
his book "Percival or the story of the Holy
Grail".*

*Paimpont Abbey
treasure.*

The Mouille-Croûte stream in the Valley of No Return.

The Arthurian Legend Centre

Comper castle, standing in a wonderful setting, is the right address for all those who want to know more about the history and legends of King Arthur and Brocéliande: there is a bookshop, exhibitions, guided visits into the forest, shows. It is highly successful.

Château de Comper-en-Brocéliande 56430 Concoret
Tel./Fax: 02 97 22 79 96

Viviane lake at Comper-en-Brocéliande.

windows and the stations of the Cross, inspired by Arthurian imagination.

Only a guided visit can explain the symbolism, desired by Father Gillard in 1942.

The Valley of No Return

One cold and sunny early morning in December, I took the path, which passes by the "Fairies' Mirror" to reach the eternal "Hostié" (house) of Viviane. This walk genuinely enchanted me. But is this really surprising? Isn't it the domain of Morgana, this fairy, the half-sister of King Arthur, who took her revenge on an unfaithful lover by keeping all fickle knights imprisoned in an invisible air bubble.

Only Lancelot, faithful to Guinevere with his perfect love, could free them, after braving a multitude of dangers.

High up, near the "hostié" rest a while on the rocky outcrops overlooking the path... close your eyes... can't you hear the echo of the horses' hooves of these gallant knights, in quest of the Holy Grail?

Barenton Fountain

This is accessible from the hamlet called Folle-Pensée, and it is here that

Merlin the sorcerer met the fairy Viviane for the first time...and fell madly in love with her. In order to attract her, and after resisting for a long time, he finally revealed to her the secrets of his powers. But it cost him dear! One day, when he was asleep near the fountain, Viviane cast a spell, waving her veil over him. When he awoke, he discovered that he was locked in a "magic" castle... where he could enjoy all earthly pleasures... but could never escape.

 Brocéliande

MORE INFORMATION?
Tourist office
Tourist office of Mauron
Place Abbé-Gillard 56430 Tréhorenteuc
Tel.: 02 97 93 05 12 — Fax: 02 97 73 80 39
Pays d'accueil de Brocéliande
37, avenue de la Libération 35380 Plélan-le-Grand
Tel./Fax: 02 99 06 86 07
Books to read: "The sacred places of Brocéliande" and "The legends of Brocéliande and King Arthur", monographs published by Ouest-France; "Brocéliande, a land born in the forest" from the same publisher.

Côtes-d'Armor
life-sized

DINAN AND THE BANKS OF THE RANCE

Dinan: one of the finest medieval cities in Brittany

Dinan, or the story of "love at first sight"... in 1968... when, as many may remember, the Spring was particularly "heated", politically speaking. As a young student of history then, in the Faculty of Arts at the university of Rennes, I made friends with several "revolutionaries" who, like myself, came from private schools (Catholic), which are numerous in Brittany. One of them had studied at the Cordeliers in Dinan and insisted on taking me to see the place where, he claimed, he had "suffered" for several years.

The ramparts, the half timbered houses and Jerzual street took my heart: that day I understood that old stones have their own soul, and I often go back to my beautiful... city of Dinan.

Two circuits organised by the local tourist office will let you appreciate all its richness.

The Ramparts circuit

Dinan's military vocation is intertwined with the origins of the town, as witnessed by the famous "Bayeux Tapestry", in which one of the scenes represents the attack on the keep of the first "castle" (in fact it was a feudal mound) by William the Conqueror, in the Year of Grace 1065.

In the Middle Ages, Dinan affirmed itself as one of the main strategic strongholds of the Duchy of Brittany.

It was very active for several centuries, and ships from Saint-Malo moored here, unloading their treasures of spices, salt, cod, tea, porcelain from China... Dinan and the surrounding region exported cereals, leather and wood, canvas and cloth... From Dinan, you can board a boat for a cruise along the Rance...or go and daydream along the towpath.

Opposite: **Plouha Cliff.**
One of the most beautiful wild footpaths of Brittany.

Stained glass window in the Saint-Malo church. The arrival of Duchess Anne of Brittany in Dinan.

The Ramparts Festival

Every two years, for two days in July, Dinan relives its best hours of the Middle Ages: jesters, dancers, jugglers, fire-eaters, buffoons and minstrels animate the narrow streets of the town, waiting for the big parade, with the inhabitants of Dinan wearing costumes of the era. In the military camp, you can watch dubbing scenes (where a new "knight" is solemnly presented with his arms) and furious attacks by heavily armed combatants. At the foot of the ramparts, there are jousting tournaments faithfully representing the atmosphere of those days when nobles and powerful lords faced each other.

The reputation of the ramparts of the town was so great that Duchess Anne talked about them as the "keys to her jewel casket".

They were built in the 13th century, and strengthened in the 14th and 15th centuries, forming an almost impregnable position. If it hadn't been for the demolition of the Brest gateway in 1880, the ramparts would have preserved their medieval aspect integrally: apart from a few breaches, they are the oldest and biggest in Brittany (2,648 metres).

The tour of the ramparts offers you the chance of strolling around this majestic enclosure nearly 3 km long, with its keep, its fourteen defensive or lookout towers and its four monumental gateways.

Leaving the tourist office, through the English Garden, you will come to the Sainte-Catherine tower, one of the oldest (13th century). Its position overlooking the Rance valley made it an excellent watchtower... and a magnificent spot these days for observing the river Rance, the valley and the port.

The Jerzual Gate (13th to 14th) is our next stopping point. It has always been the main entrance to the town.

The Beaumanoir tower built at the end of the 15th century, is the most elaborate artillery construction, a sort of "rampart sticking out like a horse-shoe", with walls 8 metres thick, like the Governor's tower.

The very pleasant walk along the moat, the Grands Fossés (15th to 18th), takes you to the Saint-Julien tower (14th) which acted as the powder store, and then the Brest gateway (14th to 15th) whose foundations have recently been rebuilt.

The walk along the Petits Fossés moat (15th to 18th), near the Beaufort tower (13th) next brings you to the Connétable tower (15th) and the keep (also called the Duchess Anne tower), which is the castle museum of Dinan. Its construction was started in 1380, by the Duke of Brittany Jean IV, while Estienne Le Fur was the

Dinan ramparts and the Duchess-Anne tower.

"*master contractor*". This was a defensive work, with the appearance of a fortress, but was also a dwelling with character, with its big windows and sculpted chimneys. It is the town museum now, and here you can discover the history of the favourite city of the Dukes of Brittany.

The Guichet Gate (13th) and that of Coëtquen (15th), together with the keep, form an ensemble which has been called the "Dinan castle" since the 16th century.

The Guichet Gate, standing at the southern entrance to medieval Dinan, has luckily kept its two enormous towers pierced with arrow slits. The circuit around the ramparts, a real tour around the very heart of the military history of the Middle Ages, ends with the Duchess-Anne Promenade, after passing by the Saint-Louis gateway (1620) and the Penthièvre tower (15th).

The Old Dinan circuit

From the tourist office, take the rue de l'Horloge (Clock Tower) to the rue du Jerzual leading down to the port, through narrow streets and alleys called the Poissonnerie, Mittrie, Cordonnerie... and Dinan will show you its marvels of wood and stone.

Rue de l'Horloge: could any more sumptuous introduction to Old Dinan exist than this magnificent dwelling,

In the Middle Ages, trading was carried out under the porches of these wood-framed houses, in Apport street, typical of the Dinan buildings from the 15th, 16th and 17th centuries: houses with overhanging upper floors, houses supported by pillars, called porch houses (16th century), and houses with windows – work of marine carpenters, with their high and wide windows facing the street, recalling the aftercastle of the royal vessels (17th century).

Bertrand du Guesclin, high constable of France

He was born in Broons (20 km south-west of Dinan) and became known very young because of his victories in chivalric tournaments. At the time of the Brittany War of Succession, he successfully defended the very prized city of Dinan, before being taken prisoner during the battle of Auray in 1364.

After the ransom for his freedom had been paid, the same year he joined the service of Charles V king of France. He liberated the country from the "Grandes Compagnies" mercenaries and the English invaders, and was killed in 1380 during the siege of Châteauneuf-du-Randon (centre of France), and had the right to... four tombs! The "heart" in the Saint-Sauveur church of Dinan, the "entrails" at Puy-en-Velay, the "flesh" in Clermont-Ferrand and the "skeleton" in the Basilica of Saint Denis near Paris, under the express order from Charles V that he should be buried with the Kings of France.

The banks of the Rance. Fisherman's hut.

the former Keratry town house (dated 1558), which is now the tourist office?

Look up and take the time to admire these houses from the 15th and 16th centuries, such as No. 35, called the "Middle Ages" house which is astonishing with a door opening directly from the first floor to the street (in fact, to simplify carrying objects which could not pass through the inside staircase); the angle statue representing Saint Nicholas (17th) was only set in place in the 1900's.

The Clock Tower, which stands with its high silhouette in the middle of the road, was erected at the end of the 15th

The Saint-Sauveur Basilica

It was built in the 12th century, by a young feudal lord of Dinan, Rivallon Le Roux. Around 1112, he went on a crusade to fight in Palestine, and during a battle whose outcome was uncertain, he made the vow that he would build a church dedicated to Saint Sauveur if he returned home alive.

When he returned he started to build a Romanesque church (around 1120), which was greatly altered over the following centuries, thus the mixing of Gothic, Classic and Baroque styles.

The Romanesque porch of the Saint-Sauveur Basilica must be admired. The "Christ in Glory" can be seen, on the tympanum (added in 1863), and especially the astonishing variety of the arch-shafts, on the theme of the capital sins: lechery, idleness, greed, gluttony... Horned devils, sirens and serpents interlaced remind the faithful of the dangers threatening them... and therefore, the need to follow the teachings of the Church.

century to act as a watchtower: as it was 30 metres higher than the ramparts patrol, it could give warning of fires (dangerous for the wooden houses of the Middle Ages)... and an advancing enemy could be spotted!

In 1498, a clock was added with a very complex mechanism, made in Nantes by a German with the name of Hamzer. As a symbol of the prosperity and power of the town, a very big bell was offered to the tower, in 1507, by Duchess Anne. A final point: from the top there is a wonderful view of the town and the Rance valley!

In the north wing of the transept is to be found the tomb enclosing the heart of Bertrand du Guesclin.

Jerzual and Petit-Fort streets

These are the genuinely old streets of Dinan, those whose old cobbles have resounded over nearly a thousand years to the passage of merchants and men at arms. They are an artery linking the port to the heart of the old town, and contributed greatly to its prosperity.

I do not know any other street in Brittany (and very few in the whole of France, apart from Sarlat, in Périgord), where stone and wood have sculpted such marvels: incontestably the "Governor's House" is the jewel (15th to 16th). It is no wonder that these days it is the home of artisans such as potters, artists, jewellers, cabinet makers...

The banks of the River Rance

The heritage built in Dinan is exceptional, and somewhat overshadows the natural riches of its surroundings. However, the banks of the Rance often offer surprises to strollers and other dreaming walkers. I have chosen two walks, in particular, from all those suggested by the tourist office.

The Châtelier walk

Leaving from the old Dinan bridge, this walk follows the right bank, as far as the Châtelier village, and then the lock of the same name. Return along the towpath following the maritime Rance: 7 km of silence, only disturbed by the songs of the birds.

The "meadow promenade" as far as Léhon

Roger Vercel, the writer from Dinan, described it so well: *"The landscape of the Rance loses its character here, because of its perfection. It is no longer a river, but 'the' river..."*

The "meadow promenade" ends at the old Léhon bridge: the green foliage marries with the grey stones, on these arches bowing under the weight of years. It replaced the ford a long time ago, the ford which was so essential to the old Roman road of Corseul-Rennes.

After the bridge, you will find the remains of a big abbey founded in the 9th century by Nominoé, king of Brittany. One day, when he was out hunting game, he met six monks and addressed them roughly as follows: *"You will receive many benefits from my royal person if you build a church to hold the relics of a saint, whom I could appeal to under any circumstances."*

The monks set off immediately for Sark (to the east of Guernsey), and "borrowed" the body of Saint Magloire, former bishop of Dol-de-Bretagne. The church which was built to shelter these precious relics attracted more and more pilgrims but, around the year 920, the Norsemen arrived and ransacked the land, ruining the prosperous abbey.

It was only at the end of the 12th century that the abbey church was built, and only the porch is practically intact these days. Late in the afternoon, when the sun's rays light up the facade, the sculpted heads of the doorway can be seen clearly, with their

Remains of Léhon Abbey.

edifying or terrifying expressions typical of the Romanesque epoch.

Continue by visiting the cloisters and the monks' refectory (13th century), the monastery buildings and the dormitories (17th), the museum and the gardens on the banks of the Rance.

The romantic ruins of the "castel" from the 12th century, perched on the heights overlooking this peaceful village built in stone, defy time... and the near ramparts of Dinan.

Inside the abbey church, you cannot fail to admire, first of all, the astonishing baptismal font from the 13th century: it is sculpted all over (these "strange" heads!), whereas its smooth and polished edges are not due to the "wear of ages" as could be thought but... to the sickles and scythes of the local peasants who used to sharpen their tools here in the hope of a good harvest.

 Dinan

MORE INFORMATION?
Tourist office of the Dinan district
6, rue de l'Horloge, BP 261, 22105 Dinan
Tel.: 02.96.87 69 76 —
Fax: 02.96.87 69 77
E-mail: infos@dinan-tourisme.com
Website: www.dinan-tourisme.com

Arrival in Paimpol bay by the customs officers' path - the GR 34. An example of a path in the wild with breathtaking viewpoints.

THE GOËLO, FROM THE PLOUHA CLIFFS TO THE LIGHTS OF BRÉHAT

One windy afternoon in the month of May, I climbed up the cliff paths from Plouha... such happiness!

Every year, Raz Point accepts nearly a million visitors; that of Plouha, a few hundred walkers. However, if I dare say so, the Costarmoricain site has just as much to offer as its namesake in Finistère. Moreover, who knows that the coastal path follows the highest cliffs in Brittany (104 metres at the top!), offering sublime views?

From Plouha to Bréhat, the Goëlo is "life-sized"... Let us begin...

Plouha

There are inspired places in Brittany, and localities with unimaginable riches. Plouguerneau, in Finistère, literally enchanted me (but this is not surprising, along this fabulous Coast of Legends). Plouha, in the Côtes-d'Armor, which shelters real marvels, amazed me.

The coastal paths and Gwin Zegal port

Between Palus beach and that of Bréhec, there are 14 km of wild coastline with the whole range of the natural charms of Brittany: rocky points and steep cliffs, deep creeks and coves with polished pebbles, a cloak of gorse and a carpet of flowers. Short walks and long treks are here for you to enjoy.

The GR 34 trail (the famous "customs officers' path") follows the length of the Goëlo coastline (and even the Côtes-d'Armor), and is the answer to all expectations of enthusiastic trekkers: from Palus beach, the path climbs up the hill, a steep ascent certainly, but so beautiful in the month of May, with the tonic air of the heath and the gorse. On the heights, the sea-fennel is encrusted in the cracks of the rocks and the sea thrift makes the cliffs rose-coloured, following one after the other up to the Bréhec cove.

Plouha Point offers one of the widest panoramas of the whole of the Channel: to the east, Saint-Brieuc bay, Erquy, Cape Fréhal; to the west the Plouézec cliffs and the Ile de Bréhat.

Beg Hastel Point ("castel") reveals the ruins of an old battery. Finally, the

GR 34 trail goes round the Tour Point before setting off for Bréhac cove, where the fine sandy beach is an invitation to a well merited rest!

Shorter walks

Plouha offers many loop circuits, accessible for everyone, for example the "Shelburn path" (3 km, 45 minutes) and "from Bonaparte beach to Gwin Zegal" (9 km, 2 hrs 30 minutes). Apart from the attraction of the wide open spaces and a nature which has been totally preserved, these walks will take you to historical sites, the "Bonaparte" beach and the Gwin Zegal port.

The famous general Shelburn never set foot on the sands of Bonaparte beach, this was simply the code name for the Cochat cove, used by the Resistance during the Second World War. Many operations for evacuating allied pilots started from here, announced by the BBC: *"Bonjour à la maison d'Alphonse."*

Led by resistants from Plouha, who knew the place perfectly (and the danger of the cliffs), twenty to twenty-five aviators collected on this beach, after avoiding the minefields, to reach the English boats waiting for them at sea, all lights extinguished.

There is a memorial on the heights recalling the heroism of the Shelburn network, whose twenty-three members paid for their courage with their lives. This is one of the twenty-four official sacred places of the French Resistance.

Near Plouha Point, the port of Gwin Zegal is only accessible by a twisty path and at the end there is an astonishing view from the rocky strand: Forty-four wooden stakes (if I am not mistaken), proudly standing up pointing to the sky.

Guilben Point. This illuminated itinerary should be taken in May or June, when perfumed by the flowering gorse.

A few fishing boats or yachts come in to moor in this very bare place: no quay and no harbour master, just a shelter, certainly protected from the fury of the winds (except from the north-west) and the big ocean waves. It is very old, and one of the last of its kind still existing in Europe and, because of this, now historically protected.

The religious heritage

Nature is beautiful in Plouha... The cultural heritage is too, with these two jewels: Lanloup church and the Kermaria an Iskuit chapel.

The latter, famous for its "Danse macabre" owes its foundation without doubt to one of the feudal lords of Plouha, Henri d'Avaugour, who set off for the crusades and returned safely in 1240. In recognition of the protection from the Virgin Mary, he built this chapel (which was modified and extended in the 15th century). The words "Kermaria an Iskuit" can be translated by "the village of Mary who protects it" or "who provides good health".

I contemplated the "Danse macabre" for a long time, after admiring the polychrome wooden statues of the apostles in the entrance porch. Marie-Josèphe, guardian and well-informed guide to this chapel of treasures which have luckily been well protected...

Plouha.
Kermaria an
Iskuit chapel.
A very beautiful
Virgin and Child
polychrome
statue.

enthusiastically described at length the other statues inside.

Plouézec

If Mother Nature favoured Plouha, she did not forget Plouézec, as I verified along the "customs officers' path" (13 km along the commune) which faithfully follows the coastline, from Bréhec beach to the Craca strand (dominated by a perfectly restored mill which operates during the season).

Beauport Abbey

In 1202 Count Alain de Penthièvre et de Goëlo began building a monastery to welcome the Premonstrants from the Normandy Abbey of Lucerne.

The grandiose remains of those days are evidence of the importance it had in the whole region in the Middle Ages. It was bought by the Coastline Conservation Trust in 1992, and is now under meticulous restoration. A few rooms and halls can already be visited, with their medieval ambience, such as the Duke's House, the cellar, the refectory, the almonery etc.

In summer, there are high quality performances here, in the image of the "stories and legends of Brittany", during the "Jeudis de Beauport".

Along this coastal path, or with other walks offered by this charming commune of Goëlo, little chapels and old flax lavoirs (wash-houses) can be discovered.

Minard and Bilfot Points offer magnificent views.

"Come and breathe the sea air" announces a local tourist document... an invitation to accept without delay!

 Beauport

MORE INFORMATION?
Abbaye de Beauport
Kerity 22500 Paimpol
Tel: 02 96 55 18 58 —
Fax: 02 96 55 18 56

Paimpol

*"I love Paimpol and its cliff
Its church and its great pardon."*

There are no cliffs at Paimpol... but nonetheless the song "La Paimpolaise" by Théodore Botrel has immortalised this famous "Icelanders' port" just like the novels of Pierre Loti.

The song still belongs to the town, as proved by the popular Sea-Shanties festival, which is greatly appreciated in the summer. Although fishing in Iceland made its fortune and its reputation, it should not be forgotten that this was a privateers' city in earlier centuries.

The "Mémoires", painted wooden plaques naming those lost at sea, fill the porch of the Perros-Hamon chapel and emphasise the heavy tribute paid to the sea by the nearby fishing village, Pors-Even. Inside, the very fine statue of Notre-Dame de Perros-Hamon, surrounded by many ex-votos, is witness of the gratitude of the sailors to their protector. They carry her aloft in a procession, on the day of the Pardon, on Easter Monday.

Paimpol and cod-fishing

From the 15th century, fishermen from Paimpol and the region set off for Iceland and Newfoundland. The peak of this activity was between 1852 and 1935: forty to fifty schooners, each with 20 to 25 men aboard, set off at the beginning of spring to return in the autumn. Between the two dates, 120 boats sank, as a victim of storms, boarding attacks or thick fog, with the loss of more than two thousand sailors.
The Maritime Museum, rue Labenne, which is located in a building where the cod used to be dried, retraces the era of these courageous seamen.

The historic centre

The "Latin quarter", a maze of narrow streets, opens onto the port: taverns and cabarets preserve the atmosphere of

Ploubazlanec.

The little Trieux train, from Paimpol to Pontrieux

Each year, from June 15th to September 15th, the steam train takes you on a very pleasant ride along the banks of the Trieux, crossing through the Penhoat-Lancerf woods, going by the Traou Nez manor (where the Seznec legal mystery still exists from the end of the twenties), with terminus at Pontrieux, the "little Venice", with its fifty delightful public wash-houses, full of flowers.

the great cod-fishing century, when the "Icelanders" returned to tell about their perilous fishing expeditions.

Martray Square has preserved beautiful dwellings from the 16th century. Pierre Loti stayed at the barrel-vaulted house at the corner of the rue de l'Eglise (in his book "Pêcheur d'Islande" his heroine Gaud lived there).

Ploubazlanec

"*Iceland, always Iceland*", wrote Pierre Loti, discovering the "Mémoires" hooked under the porch of the Perros-Hamon chapel, which he baptised the "shipwrecked chapel". Even today, Ploubazlanec still keeps the memory of the "Icelandic epoch", which left so many families in mourning.

The widows' cross

This cross, perched on the heights overlooking Pors-Even, was named this way by the writer Pierre Loti, because this is where the wives of the "Icelanders" gathered to look for the sails of the schooners returning from their fishing season. And for those whose boat did not come in, they knew they would soon have to put on widow's mourning clothes, with a big black coat, covering them from head to foot.

After a vivifying walk to Paon Point, it is pleasant to go to one of the island's pubs with a welcoming atmosphere.

Bréhat: the isle of flowers

It is an isle of flowers with a taste of Paradise, one of the rare places where one feels happy... Bréhat is one of these.

A crossing of only ten minutes, from Arcouest Point, and you are already landing at Port-Clos... and this is sheer enchantment. Goodbye to the noise and exhaust fumes of the continent; just silence and the welcoming smiles of the residents. The automobile has no rights in this Eden... and what a relief this is!

Butterfly island, set in the very middle of a myriad of tiny isles, Bréhat twinkles with a thousand sparks, like a double facetted diamond: "Mediterranean" in the south and "Irish" in the north.

"One would say it was in the South"

"An extraordinary garden", wrote the delighted poet and this is certainly the impression given by the little pathways criss-crossing the South isle, from the landing-stage of Port-Clos to Pont-Vauban. From the month of January, the heady fragrance of the mimosa is everywhere. Spring and summer see the island take on the bright colours of the agapanthus and the hydrangea, eucalyptus and fuchsia, honeysuckle and roses, rose laurel and mulberry etc.

Passing by the gardens and fields, breathe in the perfumes carried by the wind. And soon you will come to the small walls, all pink, bordering the little houses of the village. Take a welcome rest at one of the little bars and fishermen's cafés, just like at the time of the Privateers, where the bar is in fact the half-hull of a boat.

Many "Bréhatins" adventured over the seas of the globe, as can be seen from the model of the "Reder Mor" frigate in the little Paris church, owned by vice-admiral François Cornic (1731-1801), and offered by his son Yves-Marie, in 1836.

After strolling along the narrow streets, turn towards the Maudez Cross and on the way visit the Saint-Michel chapel perched at... 33 m above sea level!

The North Island, kingdom of heath and granite

Pont Vauban marks the "border", peaceful nonetheless. It is the solid proof of the arrival of this great military engineer, in 1695, to strengthen the defences of the island, in order to face up to the repeated attacks of the *"wretched English"*.

The heaths are full of the colours of heather (from April) and gorse on this windswept land. This is Brittany with an Irish touch, which reveals its harsh beauty all along the path leading to the Paon lighthouse.

The site, surrounded by enormous rocks and boulders and beaten by the furious booming tides, is especially impressive. Myself, I never dared check a tradition which young girls were supposed to follow in days gone by, hoping to discover their future in this gulf. They threw little stones

 Bréhat

MORE INFORMATION?
Information Bureau
Île de Bréhat, 22870
Tel: 02 96 20 04 15

From the Maudez Croix, there is a wonderful picture of the islands and islets (Béniguet, Croezen...) which are best seen at low tide.
The Birlot tidal mill, the recently restored magnificent "stone vessel".

The little port of Loguivy-de-la-Mer.
A gastronomic stop where you can enjoy lobsters, big crabs, spider-crabs and spiny lobsters, always freshly delivered by the many lobster boats.

down: if these fell straight into the deep without touching the rocks, they could hope to be married within the year; otherwise they would have to wait the same number of years as there were rebounds.

After the Paon lighthouse, retrace your steps to join the Rosédo path and the rock christened the Renan Chair, facing the ocean... but please don't walk over the heath at night, I promise you that I have seen thousands of little goblins dancing there!

Loguivy-de-la-Mer

"Loguivy de la mer
Loguivy de la mer
You watch them die
The last real sailors
Loguivy de la mer
At the bottom of your old port
There are layers of old carcasses
Of boats already dead".

François Budet's deep voice has immortalised this little port nestling in the mouth of the Trieux river. Why does this refrain, filled with nostalgia, haunt my memory? I cannot explain why; it is just like that... just like the happiness I feel each time I arrive (with a car, alas!) on the quays loaded with lobster pots, in this tiny haven. And I am happy to see the crates full of newly unloaded shell-fish, which will be sent to satisfy the gourmet palates of the big cities of France.

There are still many Loguivy sailors making their lives from fishing. They described to me their happiness when setting off to sea, every day, even in the grey dawns.

It seems to me that here I met people who were simply happy to be alive. I am sure of it because they never fail to smile at passing visitors. I have seen this at Gaud, which has been the port cafe... since 1876! At the end of that afternoon of May 1st, two fishermen, who had obviously forgotten that it was time to return home, asked Gaud (the familiar name of Marguerite, the smiling patron) for several sprigs of the traditional First-of-May lily of the valley, to calm the inevitable fury of their loved ones... and then they set off, arm in arm, hilarious, accompanied by the loud laughter of their fellows... I willingly complied! Thank you, Loguivy.

THE SUMPTUOUS PAINTED DECOR OF THE CÔTES-D'ARMOR CHURCHES

In 1982, restoration work began in the little church of Langast, at the heart of the Argoat, the land of woods and wild heaths. What a surprise for the specialists of the regional Historical Monuments Conservation to discover superb frescoes hidden under the whitewash!

More recently, Romanesque paintings have been uncovered in the church at Morieux, near Saint-Brieuc. The religious edifices of the Côtes-d'Armor possess a great range of frescoes and paintings from the 10th to 20th centuries. This fascinating discovery completely overwhelmed me. Follow the guide!

Langast

Ten kilometres south of the small medieval city of Moncontour, the Saint-Gal church shelters a treasure which is only known to certain specialists: Romanesque (or pre-Romanesque) frescoes which are the admiration of the most eminent professors of the history of art... nonetheless very prudent about dating them: second half of the 9th century or first half of the 10th (earliest estimate), or first half of the 12th century (latest estimate). The first hypothesis relies on certain details, such as the clothing and faces which recall certain manuscripts from the Landévennec abbey... or even from Ireland.

The angels, messengers of God, the "Creator"

The decor painted in the Langast church was conceived, just like the architecture, according to a symbolic belonging to all Romanesque churches: the angels to be seen on the arcades represent the intermediary between the divine and the earthly, between God and Man, the arcades holding up the roof and walls representing the intermediary between the sky and the earth.

The series of frescoes corresponds to the same desire for definite symbols, as emphasised by the very detailed brochure of the General Inventory dedicated to them: *"One passes from the terrestrial world represented by the foliated scrolls to the celestial world, by the intermediary of Michael, the angel of passage, and Melchisedec, figure of the perfect priest. Symbolically, there is no better way of illustrating the role of the priest, the intermediary between God and men".*

Michael and Melchisedec

Although most of the angels adopt the same position, with a closed book in the left hand and the right hand lifted with the palm facing outwards, two alone are clearly identifiable, thanks to the inscriptions: "Michael" and "Melchisedec".

Michael
How long did I stand in front of this representation of the Archangel, head of the celestial army? I cannot tell; it has never ceased intriguing me since then.
And what is the symbolism of the child he is carrying in his robes? Is it the Christ child? A soul? Melchisedec as a baby?

Melchisedec
The King of Salem, "Preacher of The Highest", contemporary of Abraham, is an astonishing composition.

Essential reading:
"Wall paintings of the Saint-Gal church, Langast", from the General Inventory, on sale in the church.

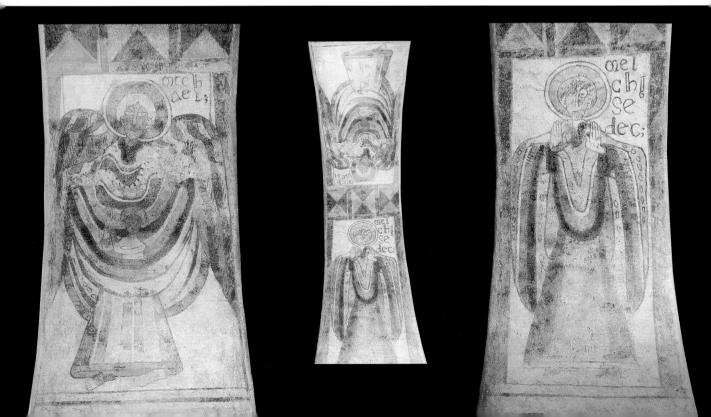

The Notre-Dame-du-Tertre paintings, in multivision

Each summer, from July 10th to August 31st, in the hall of the ex- "Petit Echo de la mode", a diaporama is projected on three screens, illuminating the paintings perfectly. Information from the tourist office.

Châtelaudren

This is a veritable "strip cartoon" with 132 scenes representing the Old and New Testaments, the legend of Sainte Marguerite and that of Saint Fiacre, designed under the vaults of the Notre-Dame-du-Tertre chapel. The style of the robes made it possible to date this masterpiece between the years 1460-1480... but unfortunately the artist is unknown!

In the chapel on the right of the choir: the life of Saint Fiacre and that of Sainte Marguerite. Thirty-six panels recount the story of these saints, highly popular in Brittany (as in France) in the Middle Ages.

Saint Fiacre

Fiacre the monk, son of the king of Hibernia (Ireland), arrived in the 7th century to Christianise the pagans, so numerous on the continent. When he met Saint Faron, bishop of Meaux (Seine-et-Marne), he asked for lands to build a monastery. In response, the latter agreed to give him all the area which he could surround with a ditch in one day.

The hermit started off immediately, dragging behind him a spade which - like magic - dug and a wide and deep trench! A (wicked) local woman "la Becnaude" who watched the scene, denounced the monk Fiacre to the bishop, seeing the work of the devil in what had happened.

The miracles worked later by this man of faith confounded "la Becnaude" and even Faron implored pardon from... the future patron saint of gardeners!

Sainte Marguerite

Just like the "life of Saint Fiacre", there are eighteen panels illustrating the "life of Sainte Marguerite", according to the well-known legend from the 12th century. She is said to have lived in Antioch (Turkey) in the 3rd century,

The wainscoting in the choir. Ninety-six little panels illustrate the Old and New Testaments, from the Creation of the Earth until Pentecost: the Bible in marvellous images, for the faithful. From the "Creation of Light and the Angels", the first, to "Pentecost", the descent of the Holy Spirit on the disciples, the last, a lesson in religion... with the clothing, objects and tools of the 15th century!

 Châtelaudren Chapelle Notre-Dame-du-Tertre

MORE INFORMATION?
Guided visits of the chapel are available in July-August: address enquiries to the tourist office of Chatelaudrun, tel: 02 96 74 12 02.
To read: "The Notre-Dame-du-Tertre chapel", a very detailed work, well illustrated and published by the Châtelaudren town hall.

Danse macabre in the Kermaria chapel in Isquit. The dance, expression of joy and happiness, transforms into a deadly saraband, to the rhythm of the alternation of a skeleton pulling a figure of lowly or the highest estate: knight, bishop, constable, king, cardinal, emperor, pope. The message is clear: none can escape death. A message inscribed in gothic letters above each figure emphatically claims this fact, such as the text concerning the pope:

"What? does the dance have to involve
The guarantor of God on earth?
My dignity was sovereign Over the church like Saint Peter.
It is too early to bury me. But, like others, I trespassed. Death makes war against everyone: Honour does nothing: it vanishes."

and was sent away by her father Edesius, a pagan high-priest. She took refuge with her nurse who brought her up in the Christian faith.

Olibrius, governor of the province, fell in love with the beautiful and pure young girl, who had become a shepherdess... but she refused his advances! He took his revenge by submitting her to a series of torments... which she resisted victoriously. Just before being beheaded, she beseached God to help those women in childbirth who called upon him.

The "life of Sainte Marguerite", wonderfully illustrated in Châtelaudren, was greatly appreciated in the Middle Ages, especially by pregnant women, many of whom tried to procure the 'Sainte Marguerite girdle", thought to help their delivery.

The Plouha "Danse Macabre"

The "Kermaria an Isquit" chapel ("the house of Mary who gives good health"), has one of the five great "Danse Macabre" still existing in France. It dates from the

Saint-Gonery chapel in Plougrescant: creation of the world.

very end of the 15th century and is an exceptional testimony of the fear of death in France and Europe at the end of the Middle Ages, faced with the terrible epidemics of the plague.

This "Danse Macabre" takes its inspiration from a fresco on the walls of the Saints-Innocents cemetery in Paris.

The painted vaulting of the Saint-Gonery chapel in Plougrescant

Some art historians attribute a certain "naivety" to the Saint-Gonery paintings (dated back to the 16th century), in comparison with the "finesse" of those of Châteaudren. I do not agree at all myself: listen to your heart, and feel your emotion, in front of these scenes from Genesis, the Old and the New Testaments (the Nativity, the Presentation at the Temple, the Betrayal of Judas etc.).

plans of James Bouillé, was the result of the joint talents of the artists from the Christian Breton Art Workshop, working together like the building brotherhoods of the Middle Ages. According to Denise Delouche, emeritus professor of art history, the interior painted by Xavier de Langlais is a *"summit of religious decoration"*. The Stations of the Cross as depicted by this dedicated defender of Brittany is certainly among the most beautiful of the seven which he painted in other churches (such as Mérillac and Plounevez-Quintin in the Côtes-d'Armor).

Saint-Joseph of Lannion. A "modern" art treasure in Brittany, to be cared for.

The Stations of the Cross at Lannion

The Saint-Joseph chapel, constructed between 1936 and 1937, following the

Lannion
Chapelle Saint-Joseph

MORE INFORMATION?
Guided visits are available each summer, organised by the Lannion tourist office, quai d'Aiguillon, 22300 Lannion
Tel: 02 96 46 41 00 — Fax: 02 96 37 19 64
To read: "Xavier de Langlais et la Bretagne", a work produced under the direction of Denise Delouche, Published by Coop-Breizh

Finistère
a land of character

THE HUELGOAT FOREST AND THE ARRÉE MOUNTAINS: THIS INNER BRITTANY

I celebrated my half-century in the Youdig inn, in the shadow of the Brennelis nuclear power plant (closed down these days), together with very dear friends. The generous "Kig ha farz" (a rich Breton stew) and the Breton dances improvised so enthusiastically by the cook and the waitress easily helped me to forget the weight of years!

I love the Arrée mountains. In 1977, in the company of my young wife, I crossed them... on foot... meeting a few amazed tourists on the way. In those days, hiking was not yet in fashion. These days it has developed enormously, on these eroded mountains, just as in the forest of Huelgoat, the refuge of King Arthur... and so many fairies!

We are now in the heart of the Argoat, the "realm of woods", that of secret Brittany. Welcome to the kingdom of goblins.

Huelgoat and its forest

"The more I think about Huelgoat, the more I understand that I only glimpsed the surface of its marvels which are still unexplored and untouched", wrote Paul Sérusier, a well-known artist from the Pont-Aven school. We shall follow his inspiration, making our way along the "picturesque path", the green Ariane thread.

The "picturesque path"

What an uninspiring name for a path bordered with so many exciting spots! After taking only a few steps, you enter the realm of the extraordinary, at the Chaos du Moulin (Mill Rocks), a ducal mill built in 1339, and taken over by the Mining Company of Lower Brittany in the 18th century. It now belongs to the Armorique Regional Nature Park, which organises exhibitions here in the summer.

The "chaos", gigantic rocks piled

Opposite:
A colourful scene: unloading crawfish in Guilvinec.
It happens every day
(or almost) at the end
of the afternoon.

The Argent river in the heart of the Huelgoat forest.

those from Plouyé (5 km south of Huelgoat). Encouraged by their respective guiding spirits, each side tried to crush the enemy under a deluge of rocks...which landed at Huelgoat... half way between them.

Leave the rocks to climb down a few metres to the Devil's Grotto. Here, the river goes underground. It is reached by a simple iron rail, a frail protection in this "demonic" site... which has given rise to another legend. But, for once, it does not owe its name to Satan, but to a "Blue", a partisan of the Revolution and a native of nearby Berrien. He was being pursued by his enemies, the Royalist "Chouans", and took refuge here. Since it was very cold, he lit a big fire using branches. Wearing his hat

The abyss and the legend of Dahut

By following Violette alley (so-called because the engineer Violette traced it out), alongside the river d'Argent, or by the departmental road 769, you will reach this abyss, where the water sometimes seems to take on a strange "blood-red" colour.

According to legend, it is the blood of lovers thrown into the river by Dahut, the cruel princess of Ys. She was the daughter of king Gradlon, and led a dissipated life in this city, as well as in her castle of "Kastell Ar Guibel" built on the cliff overlooking the abyss. Each night she chose a lover from among the most handsome young men, and then before dawn she (or her faithful servants) threw him into the racing waters.

But in the end Dahut had to pay for her crimes: when the town of Ys was flooded, through her fault, she was transformed into a siren by Saint Guénolé and passed through an underground passage down to the abyss, to cover the cries of her poor lovers with her song.

The rocks have taken on strange forms, carved out by the running waters, and with a little (or even a lot) of imagination, you can make out the "Spoon", the "Bellows", the "Butter Churn", the "Cauldron", the "Umbrella", the "Armchairs" and even the "Bed" of the Virgin!

here and there along the river d'Argent, can be explained by the phenomenon of erosion, according to scientists. But there are several legends giving other versions. The first claims that this "chaos" was the work of the giant Gargantua: "*Stopping at Huelgoat one day to satisfy his huge appetite, he asked the inhabitants for something to eat... but they only gave him a poor rye soup.*

He was very angry and left immediately, deciding to take his revenge. He came to Léon country, seized the biggest rocks he could find, polished since the dawn of time by the ocean, and tossed them over the Arrée mountains onto the Huelgoat and its forest... where they still lie in large numbers."

The second tale insists that these piles of rocks are the result of a bitter battle between the former giants of Berrien (5 km north of Huelgoat) and

Huelgoat

MORE INFORMATION?
Tourist office,
BP 19, 29690 Huelgoat
Tel: 02 98 99 72 32 —
Fax: 02 98 99 75 72

with its two red feathers sticking out he waited for his adversaries, standing firm with a big fork in his hand. When the Chouans came down into the grotto they thought they saw the shadow of Satan behind the fire and fled shouting: "The Devil, the Devil!"

From **Ménage**, climb the steps leading you to the **Roche tremblante**, or Logan Stone. This enormous block of stone 7 metres long and 3 metres high, weighing nearly 140 tons, rocks easily

*The "Virgin's Household",
a site ready for any legend.*

(so they say!) by simply leaning against it at a special point... which has yet to be discovered.

The "picturesque path" ends at the Red bridge, which is the departure point for other paths through the forest.

The Wild Boar pool

By following the well-named "Clear Stream" alley, you will easily find the beautiful "Wild Boar pool". The still waters where the many wild boar who roamed this huge forest used to drink, opens the door these days to the realm of dreams and contemplation.

Arthur's camp

This authentic Celtic oppidum (a fortified place where the people used to take refuge) has been given the name of the famous king of Brittany, whose exploits are recounted in the tales about the Knights of the Round Table. The memory of this fabulous hero haunts the forest, as proved by another mythical site, near to the "Artus camp".

Arthur's cave

Legend has it that the king slept here, in the company of his faithful companions. Woe to those who went

The Wild-Boar pool.

"The Argoat garden"

Originally, this was a medicinal garden in the grounds of the hospital centre of Huelgoat. These days, thanks to the director's passion for plants with a risk of becoming extinct, it is a real botanical park open to the public. Its paths, each with a theme, reveal a thousand carefully documented species. This "Garden of Eden" is also enriched by an arboretum of 45 acres, containing 2,500 species of trees and bushes from the five continents.

The Argoat garden

MORE INFORMATION?
Jardin de l'Argoat
55, rue des Cieux 29690
Huelgoat
Tel: 02 98 99 71 63
Arboretum du Poërop
29690 Huelgoat
Tel: 02 98 99 95 90

into the cave and awoke him without good reason: they never came out again alive. But one day, when his country was in danger, Arthur awoke to save the kingdom of Brittany.

A second legend tells us that this cave hides a treasure discovered in the Vale of No Return, (in Brocéliande forest) by King Arthur, thanks to Merlin the sorcerer. But take care, it is guarded by terrifying demons flying through the air in the form of elves... little malicious goblins which can do so much harm!

Offerings of manes and tails of horses and cows at Saint-Herbot.

Plonevez-du-Faou: Saint-Herbot chapel

This cathedral of granite, a huge stone vessel stranded at the foot of the Arrée mountains seems, over the years, to have defied the ravages of time, and any understanding: why was such a monument built in a hamlet with only a few houses, even though

they are so attractive?

Once again, the answer comes from the privileged position of Saint-Herbot, which in the Middle Ages was a very busy crossroads between Léon, Cornouaille and Poher. Big fairs used to be held here. Taxes and gifts from the faithful greatly contributed to building this masterpiece of Breton Renaissance architecture.

Work began on July 1st 1498, witnessed by the inauguration stone of the South Porch, and ended in 1556, according to the date marked beneath the

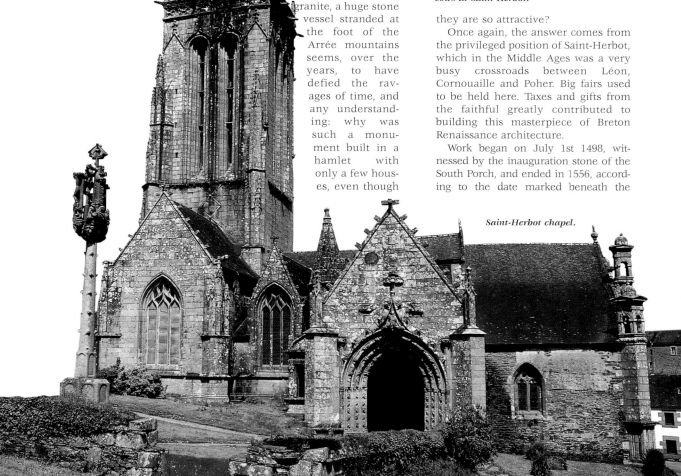

Saint-Herbot chapel.

stained glass windows. The external architecture is remarkable (and especially the tower which is very impressive, 30 metres high!). The inside shelters sheer marvels: the central window illustrates the Passion of Christ (work of Thomas Quemener, the master artist in stained glass from Morlaix); the chancel and the crucifixion dominating it; the statues including those of Saint Yves and Saint Corentin; the Pietà with angels group, in polychrome white stone (beginning of the 16th century), recently restored and allowing all of its beauty to be admired (believe me, even this alone is worth coming to see); the arches against the wall in the Sainte-Barbe chapel...

The calvaries in the Parish closes are quite rightly famous... That of Saint-Herbot, built in 1575, just in front of the South Porch, is just as wonderful. It needed genius to sculpt the Kersanton granite with so many scenes from the Passion of Christ and these symbols of Good and Evil, and also, under the impenitent thief, these demons, one looking like a vampire.

Read "Saint-Herbot revisited", the booklet on sale in this chapel, where enthusiastic guides officiate.

The Arrée Mountains

Amongst the blue mists
I shall leave without a word
For the marshes of Yeun-Elez
I shall slide myself
Into the sad lands of Botmeur,
Tears making the stones smooth.
I shall leave without any curse
Silent, useless, without eyelids
Into the uselessness of the bogs.

Xavier Grall,
"Sound of rain and tombs".

The tourist may not be attracted by the desolate solitude of the Arrée mountains, but the genuine visitor will find fulfilment. The peat-bogs and the heaths reign here... The wind and the rain have shaped needles of schist tearing apart these mountains beaten by the ages: Roc'h Trévezel, Roc'h Trédudon, Roc'h Glaz...

The Arrée mountains, grand and wild, will only reveal their secret beauty to hikers who can take their time, they are the only ones able to appreciate the infinite serenity.

In the gloomy days of winter you can appreciate the atmosphere of legend and mystery emanating from these rocks torn by the rain and the wind.

Circuits for short walks around Yeun Elez

The six communes surrounding the Yeun Elez bog and the Armorique Regional Nature Park have organised a network of 150 kilometres of marked paths... Fresh air is ensured!

• *CIRCUIT DU MENE (18 km) Leave from Brasparts (village hall). After crossing through the Isle wood, this path climbs up to the heaths at the foot of the Mont-Saint-Michel and then descends through the woods and pastures to the Chapel of the Cross (16th century).*
To return to Brasparts, the circuit follows the track of the former Plouscat-Rosporden railway line, formerly called the "potato train".

• *CIRCUIT DU YEUN (16 km) Leave from the play area near the Nestavel dam. The path makes the tour of the Saint-Michel lake which is at the centre of the Yeun Elez depression. This vast peat basin represented the gates of hell for the elders. These days, this fragile site attracts walkers because of its natural riches.*

• *CIRCUIT DU ROC'H BICHOUREL (8 km) Leave from the Botmeur town hall. This circuit mainly crosses a landscape of heaths and follows the path of the schist ridges, the natural limit separating the Léon and Cornouaille lands. Return to the town by a pretty little route offering many view-points.*

• *CIRCUIT DE ROC'H AR BIC (17 km) Leave from La Feuillée, (Marronniers Square). This circuit, taking you through the granite hills, will open up a landscape of woods and pastures reached along magnificent paths. You will cross little streams and villages with traditional houses.*

• *CIRCUIT DU RUSQUEC (10 km) Leave from Loqueffret. This path takes you to Saint-Herbot, dominated by the impressive square tower of its church. Continue along a little road passing near Rusquec manor. Then rejoin the GR at the foot of the bridge crossing the river Elez. Then take the path leading back to the station and town of Loqueffret.*

...

Brennilis and the Yeun-Elez peat bogs

Brennilis, at the gates of Hell... Without the enormous iron and steel structures of the power station disfiguring the landscape, Brennelis would look the same as any other Arrée village... yes, but here, according to tradition, there is one of the Gates to Hell, the "youdig". Alas, man has ransacked the sacred site, the "Yeun Elez" marshes, which formerly were reserved for the errant souls of the dead, and where, they say, one can see a man and his horses swallowed up by the bog.

In order to enter this dreamlike world of the Arrée mountains, I suggest a long hike, all around the Yeun Elez, between heaths and peat-bogs (16 kilometres).

The peat bogs, the humid lungs of the region, are full of cotton grass, a rare and protected northern plant.

A ray of sunshine on Trévezel rock, waiting for the "squall" ...

...

Brennilis, a land of legends... our next stop, at the "Ti ar Boudiked" (elf house) fully justifies this reputation. But never go there in the evening because, according to legend, these little creatures come out at dusk to capture travellers who dare to adventure into these Arrée mountains, to make them dance in endless rings.

Would you like more stories and fables? Then make your way to the Youdig inn (path indicated from the town) where Claude will lead you into the realm of dwarfs, night fairies or the Death figure Ankou! (Tel. 02 98 99 62 36)

• *CIRCUIT DE SAINT-RIVOAL/TRO SANT RIVOAL (16 km) Leave from the town of Saint-Rivoal. The path leads to a little pinewood and then crosses through the village of Bodenna and after that winds its way in the heath at the foot of Mont-Saint-Michel. It passes close to the sources of the Elez to reach the north of the commune and then descends back to Saint-Rivoal in the woodlands. There are magnificent views over the Rivoal valley.*

• *CIRCUIT OF HEATHS AND PEAT BOGS (14 km) Leave from the crossing of the road RN 785 and the trail GR 380-37. There is a parking place at the Artisans' House. This circuit is planned for discovering especially interesting ecological sites: the peat bog (Yeun Elez), the humid and dry heaths, the foot of the rocky outcrops (Menez Kador, Mont-Saint-Michel). The flora and fauna of these sites are fragile, so please be careful and attentive to the environment.*

 Arrée Mountains

TOPO-GUIDES AND INFORMATION
Armorique Regional Nature Park
15, place aux Foires, BP 27, 29590 Le Faou
Tel: 02 98 81 90 08

The Brasparts Calvary. Built during the first half of the 16th century, this Calvary is special because of the precision of the scenes sculpted in the black granite, representing "Saint Michael killing the dragon", on the main shaft and an unusual Pietà, under the hard and fixed gaze of three women.

Brasparts

Try it, say "Brasparts" very loud! The two syllables will give a sound as rough as the Roc'h surrounding it. This very old commune, perched on the windy heights, has kept the memory of the terror of earlier days, approaching the Yeun Elez.

Ankou *"the death worker"* reigns here, as you will discover in the Parish close, in the town of Brasparts. Although it may not have the reputation of Saint-Thégonnec or Lampaul-Guimiliau, to mention only two famous examples, nonetheless the calvary, the ossuary and the church have several singularities.

The ossuary, in characteristic flamboyant gothic, reminds the living of the precariousness of life: Ankou

Mélusine, Morgana...? Find out under the entrance porch of Brasparts church.

A saying from the Arrée mountains

According to a saying, there are miracles which God, however powerful he may be, cannot perform:
Pèder zra impossubl da Zoué :
Plénad Brazpartz ; diradèma Plouyé ;
Diveïna Berrien
Ha dic'basna Poullaouen.
There are four things impossible for God:
He cannot flatten Brazparz; pull out the ferns from Plouyé;
Remove the stones from Berrien;
And make the girls of Poullaouen chaste.

brandishes a javelin, with his terrible threat: *"I shall kill all of you."* The angel of the Resurrection replies: *"Awaken."*

At the entrance to the church, in the South Porch, there are grotesque and monster-like beings carved in the granite, under the base of the

special places of Brittany. Once again, I can only try to describe the moments of happiness spent walking these footpaths. At least get out of your car to climb up these gentle slopes, and from the summit you will see Cornouaille and the Léon... and even the Brest roadstead when the sky is clear.

The Cornec house

Just outside Saint-Rivoal, stands the grand house of "messire" Yvon Cornec, dating back to 1702. It was restored a few years ago, to become an open-air museum of the Arrée mountains. Its projecting front wing and its external staircase under a roof are typical of the dwellings of the rich peasants of the region, between the 17th and 18th centuries.

Commana, Saint-Derrien church. Detail from the Saint-Anne altarpiece.

statues of the apostles, recalling the ferocious struggle between the Catholic religion and the occult gods and forces, so present in these places.

Saint-Rivoal
This little commune, created in 1925, in the heart of the Armorique Nature Park, is a pleasure for walking enthusiasts, arriving along the footpaths which converge on the "sacred mountain" of the Arrée mountains: the Saint-Michel mountain and chapel.

From the summit, there is a vast panorama over to the distant horizon, with the Yeun Elez peat bog, below.

Commana
From the Saint-Michel-de-Brasparts chapel in Commana, the D 785 twists around the foot of the Arrée needles: "Tuchen Kador" (Toussaine beacon) and "Roc'h Trévezel". A path along the peaks links all these

After Commana, I have two very vivid memories: one is the best "Kig ha Farz" which I ever tasted, Chez Germaine who, alas, has now closed. The other came unexpectedly from the old rector, Claude Chapalain while I was admiring the extraordinary altarpieces of the Saint-Derrien church, together with some friends. He enthusiastically explained to us, in great detail, all the wealth and complexity of their symbolism.

There is a monumental porch decorated with acanthus foliage leading into this building, drowned like so many others under the grey severity of the granite. The contrast is even more striking when you go inside: in the chancel the Sainte Anne altarpiece has been shining brightly, under its baroque gilding and gold, since the year 1682.

Did the parishioners finance such a marvel to atone for some terrible sin? According to tradition, it is said that they had lynched their rector, suspecting him of betraying the "peasant code", set out after the

The Kerouat mills

Hidden in a valley dug out by the river Stain, a tributary of the Elorn, at the limit of the parishes of Sizun and Commana, the village of the Kerouat mills is a living memory of the family who lived here until the middle of the 20th century. The hamlet is made up of about fifteen buildings, the first ones dating back to the 17th century, and is now an open-air museum of the Arrée mountains.

The descendants of Derrien Fagot who died in 1806, were millers and also fodder farmers, and later horse-breeders. They organised their buildings and adapted them over two centuries to correspond to their needs. You can understand the life of five generations of millers through these houses, mills, ovens, fountains, wash-houses and a pool spread over 15 acres.

The Kerouat mills

MORE INFORMATION?
Moulins de Kerouat
29450 Commana
Tel: 02 98 68 87 76

Which is the highest point in Brittany?

Geographers and scientists have been arguing bitterly over this important subject for years: so which is the highest point in Brittany? Some say gallantly that it is the summit of Tuchen Kador (383 m); others claim that it is Roc'h Trevezel (383 m)... without doubt. And if the presence of the big aerial of a television relay could give us the name of the winner, then it is Roc'h Trédudon (385 m)... evidently!

P.S. This is simply my own personal opinion!

Arrée

MORE INFORMATION?
Tourist country of the closes and Arrée mountains
12, avenue Foch
29400 Landivisiau
Tel: 02 98 68 48 84
Pays d'accueil touristique of central Finistère
Kavarno
29520 Saint-Goazec
Tel: 02 98 26 82 02 —
Fax: 02 98 26 81 56
The association Au fil du Queffleuth et de la Penzé proposes discovery outings day or night, guided walks, sometimes with songs and stories.
The association Au fil du Queffleuth et de la Penzé
Espace Parmentier
29410 Pleyber-Christ
Tel: 02 98 78 45 69
Aufilduqueffleuth.
penze@libertysurf.fr

revolt of the Red Bonnets in 1675. He was left for dead, but nonetheless managed to survive and never reported the affair. They say that, as a pardon, this masterpiece was offered, and Claude Chapalain has made a close study of it, to be found in the work "Commana, a jewel among Breton church closes" (publishers Coop-Breizh).

The Rosaire and Cinq Plaies altarpieces also deserve your attention, as does the splendid baptistry from the 17th century.

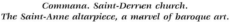

Commana. Saint-Derrien church.
The Saint-Anne altarpiece, a marvel of baroque art.

Le Pays Bigouden
Ar Vro Vigoudenn

BIGOUDEN COUNTRY,
THE LAND OF SAILORS

*"A Breton on each sod of earth,
A Breton on each wave at sea."*

These words from Victor Hugo whose mother was from Brittany, and which are so true, came back to me when I was leaning over the terrace above the fish auction of Guilvinec, watching the fishing boats coming back in.

They leave at dawn and return in the afternoon, their holds filled with fresh fish, still alive, giving out an iodised

Sainte-Marine, an adorable little port just as it should be...

Bénodet cove, at the limits of Bigouden country, a landscape dear to the regretted sailor Eric Tabarly.

Above: **Ile-Tudy. This is the kingdom of the gentle life and idleness: small fishermen's houses with blue shutters, vast beaches of fine sand. Fearful of creating another "Saint-Tropez"... we shall say no more.**

Above right: **The sailors' shelter at Sainte-Marine. Witness to the maritime heritage of Brittany, these shelters are a homage to Jacques de Thézac, the sailors' benefactor.**

perfume to bring saliva to the mouths of anaemic spirits. "The Arvorig" then "The Guerveur" unloaded their crates of squirming crawfish, sole, conger eels, monkfish, cod... under the envious eye of a few curious onlookers. Just like them, I watched the auction, hypnotised, a few minutes later: the auctioneer ("le crieur") juggled with prices and species, terminating the purchase by throwing down a coin... An astonishing spectacle, and quite incomprehensible without the explanations of an accomplished guide.

From the banks of the Odet to Audierne Bay, from Sainte-Marine to Pors-Poulhan, all turned towards the sea, the Bigouden country is sailors' land.

Sainte-Marine and Ile-Tudy

"You only need to cross the bridge..."
So sang the poet (George Brassens in this case). And there is a bridge, the Cornouaille bridge, which marks the beginning of Bigouden country. But let

us flee from the bustle of Bénodet, a well known resort, to take refuge in this tiny port admirably protected from the ocean swell and winds.

This calm and peaceful haven, very popular among pleasure boats these days, used to be a fishing port, as the "Abri du Marin" reminds us, its pink walls clashing with the white of the houses and the bar-restaurants.

"Carpe Diem" (Seize the day)... It takes a certain amount of courage to leave these quays, where you can take time to daydream... but walking called me; and I set off on the customs officers' path, towards Combrit Point and the Ile-Tudy, a very gentle hike which revealed two types of buildings along the coasts of Brittany: those which were fortified and those which sheltered the customs officers.

The fort of Sainte-Marine, built in 1861, has high crenellated walls; a little further on, the house which is (curiously) named "Ty Napoleon" seems to be somewhat abandoned and yet its granite stepped roofing is evidence that its vocation was a customs officers' shelter, like so many in the 18th and 19th centuries.

Pont-l'Abbé

This historic capital of Bigouden country, a prosperous market town, comes to life especially on Thursdays, market day: stroll along the stalls of République Square or Gambetta Square and you will certainly come across the last of the "Bigoudènes" proudly wearing their famous lace head-dresses. Is this the persistence of a folklore about to disappear, as certain grumblers say? Myself, I see more of a clear affirmation of a deep identity: the Bigouden... and the Bigoudène have character!

And this does not date from these days, as witnessed by the observations of Jean-François Bourmiche, attentive observer of the populations of Finistère in the 19th century: *"The peasants of Pont-l'Abbé come from a strong and vigorous 'race'. The men on the coast are tall, with wide shoulders, muscled chests and a proud and strong look..."*

The "Red Bonnets" circuit

This historic and tourist circuit, about 40 km long, leaving from Pont-l'Abbé, leads you to discover the main religious buildings, evidence of the famous Red Bonnets revolt, whose origins are explained below.

In 1675, the king of France Louis XIV wanted to impose new taxes on the Bretons on official stamped paper, pewter plates and tobacco. The uprising began on June 23rd 1675, at the church of Combrit, when the faithful killed the lord of Cosquer, after a Sunday mass. The whole of Lower Brittany rose up, and this was the stamped paper revolt, called the "Red Bonnets revolt", from the fact that the rebels recognised each other because they wore caps of this colour.

A "peasants' code" claiming more justice was proclaimed in the Tréminou chapel on July 2nd. The resulting repression was ferocious: thus the Duke of Chaulnes, governor of Brittany, "decapitated" the belfries of rebel parishes: Lambour, Combrit (rebuilt a century later), Lanvern and Languivoa en Ploneour.

At Pont-l'Abbé, don't miss the Le Minor house where you will find everything you could wish for dressing your table, and where it is possible to appreciate the work of Bigouden embroiderers. Seen here, Jean-Michel Perennec, working on a contemporary banner.

The Bigoudène head-dress

There is a legend (which still persists) that the Bigoudènes decided to wear high head-dresses after the repression of the Red Bonnets revolt: "The Duke of Chaulnes decided to decapitate our belfries, so now we shall carry them on our heads!"

In fact, these head-dresses were only raised after 1920, to reach 30 or 35 cm in 1940. There were still 273 women in 1993 wearing them at a gathering at Pont l'Abbé, immortalised by a poster on sale at the tourist office. Since then, Jeanne, Berthe and Maria have become real "stars" under the influence of certain advertisements on French television.

59

The historical Pont-l'Abbé circuit

This circuit, proposed by the tourist office, follows the narrow streets and reveals the main buildings and monuments of the town:

- *The former moats of the castle of the Pont barons.*
- *The church of Notre-Dame-des-Carmes, former chapel of the convent founded in 1383 (a superb rose window dating from the beginning of the 15th century).*
- *The monument to the Bigoudens, on the Saint-Laurent quay, represents three generations of Bigoudènes paying their respects to their sailors who perished at sea. It was inaugurated on September 7th 1931, and is the work of the sculptor François Bazin. There are many ideas for strolls and walks from Pont-l'Abbé: the river towpath is especially appreciated, and the most courageous continue as far as Loctudy (18 km there and back).*

The choir of Saint-Tudy church, very similar to Landevennec and Saint-Gildas de-Rhuys, has the merit of helping us imagine these two buildings which have now disappeared: curved arcades, ambulatory and rayonnant chapels, pillar capitals with vegetal decor.

 Pont-l'Abbé

MORE INFORMATION?
Tourist office
10, place de la République
29120 Pont-l'Abbé
Tel: 02 98 82 37 99 —
Fax: 02 98 66 10 82
E-mail :
otsipontlabbe@altica. com
To read: "The routes of discovery, Pont l'Abbé and surroundings", a booklet available at the tourist office.

Pierre-Jakez Hélias, the author of the "Horse of Fride" confirms: *"We other Bigoudens have the reputation of being different from the rest of the world. It must be true, since everyone says so. And us first of all."*

The ruins of the Saint-Jacques-de-Lambour church, on the left bank of the river, bear the tragic evidence of the strong character of the Bigoudens, which was marked especially in 1675 during the Red Bonnets revolt.

Notre-Dame-de-Lambour, then a subparish of Combrit (where the insurrection started) was built around 1280 and then changed considerably at the beginning of the 16th century, as its flamboyant style facade shows. Its 13th century pillars and its fine arcades emphasise the influence of the "Pont-Croix school".

The castle (Bigouden museum)

This 13th century castle was built by the lords of the Pont (Bridge), intended to be a fortress. Its was pillaged and burned down during the Red Bonnets revolt, and now houses the Bigouden museum with its rich collections of furniture and costumes... and headdresses of course.

Loctudy

"Loc Tudy" (the sacred Tudy) facing the Ile-Tudy peninsula is yet another proof of the arrival of the saints coming to Christianise the Armorique, at the time of the great migrations (between the 5th and 8th centuries).

The Saint-Tudy church is one of the best preserved Romanesque edifices in Brittany. It was built between the 11th and 12th centuries, following a plan close to that of Saint-Benoît-sur-Loire, and is bathed throughout by diffused light, giving glimpses of remarkable pillar capitals.

The Kerazan manor can be visited: within its venerable walls (16th to 18th century), the way of life of a noble family from the Second Empire has been reconstituted. The museum also displays paintings from various epochs (from the 16th to the 20th centuries) and above all, a splendid collection of Alfred Beau faience.

But first and foremost, Loctudy is a port, and in addition it is the leading port in France for fishing sardines, the famous "*Loctudy maidens*". In the summer, at 6 o'clock in the morning, Pierre Coquet, a former fisherman, will take you to discover the "criée" or fish auction, and then visit a deep-sea trawler and a store for the daily catch: two hours among the fascinating life of the sailors' universe, for a very modest sum: 10 francs which goes to the SNSM (National Lifeboat Association).

Ruins of the Saint-Jacques-de-Lambour church.

Guided visits in the fishing ports of Bigouden country

Loctudy, Plobannalec-Lesconil, Le Guilvinec-Lechiagat and Saint-Guénolé-Penmarch have several dozen boats which ensure the basis of the national market of fresh products from the sea.

The emblem of the Bigouden fishing ports is the live langoustine (Norway lobster), unloaded every evening by the coastal trawlers. They are fished during the day in the Grande Vasière zone, and the pink crustaceans are placed in tanks with seawater circulating through, to keep them alive.

At 6 o'clock in the morning or at 5 p.m. the fish is auctioned (the criée): the prices are lowered until someone buys them, or raised when there are several buyers. Each sign, whether a wink or a nod corresponds to a bid. There is a drawing of lots if several buyers reach the same final bid which they will not exceed.

 Guided visits in the fishing ports

WHERE TO FIND INFORMATION?

For the times and charges of guided visits, ask the tourist offices:
• *Loctudy: 02 98 87 53 78*
• *Plobannalec-Lesconil: 02 98 87 86 99*
• *Guilvinec-Lechiagat: 02 98 58 29 29*
• *Saint-Guénolé-Penmarch: 02 98 58 81 44*

Le Guilvinec

Between Loctudy and Guilvinec, there is a string of beaches with fine sand and very active little ports along the coast: Lesconil (the wonderful shellfish platter of the Dunes hotel!), Léchiagat (les Brisants, an authentic fishermen's bar on the quays)...

And now we have come to Guilvinec, the leading French port for non-industrial fishing. Who remembers today that in the 19th century, it was only a hamlet depending on the Plomeur commune? It was only the decree of April 6th 1880 which turned Le Guilvinec into a completely autonomous commune. What a difference a century makes!

Penmarch

"Despite all my long voyages, nothing prepared me for the idea of the ocean beating the rocks of Penmarc'h; the thick clouds of vapour twist and turn, and the sky and the sea are indistinguishable. In such a dense mist you can only glimpse enormous swells of spray; they rise, break and fly in the air with a terrifying noise; you imagine you can feel the earth trembling..."

In his "Travels in Finistère" Cambry thus described his vision of a storm in Penmarch, at the end of the 18th century. Perhaps he saw this apocalyptic spectacle at the enormous Saint-Guénolé "Rocks". Penmarch, the prow figure of the Bigouden lands, has an unusual history, and several pages are luckily inscribed in the granite of the religious buildings of its four main quarters: Kerity, Penmarch bourg, Saint-Pierre and Saint-Guénolé.

Kerity

Who could imagine that this was the leading port of Brittany in the 15th and 16th centuries, when strolling down its narrow alleys ?

But there are several facts and figures marking its flourishing prosperi-

The impressive fishing fleet of Bigouden country. It warms the heart to see it!

The Saint-Nonna church, the "cathedral of the seas", as it is called locally, stands majestically in the town of Penmarc'h. It was built in 1508 and benefited fully from the donations of the rich traders and ship-owners of Penmarc'h, as can be seen from the many "caravels" and "carracks" sculpted in bas-relief on the porch and the outside walls, on the South side.

Haliotika, the centre for discovery and interpretation of sea fishing

Haliotika, opened in March 2000, opens the doors of the marine universe, under its most varied facets. It applies the latest exhibition techniques; and you can therefore distinguish between a trawler and a net-layer, a sardine boat and a lobster boat, and discover the fishing zones, life aboard, and follow the fish, from the sea to your plate...

 Haliotika

MORE INFORMATION?
Haliotika
Terrasse panoramique de
la criée, BP 14,
29730 Le Guilvinec
Tel: 02 98 58 28 38 —
Fax: 02 98 58 98 99

Torche Point

- *The water-skiers' paradise*
"Beg an Dorchen" (cushion point) is known throughout the world these days
under the name Torche Point. It is recognised as one of the best "spots" in Europe
for surfers and fun-boarders, who arrive in increasing numbers to enjoy the
thrills of the waves which have earned it its reputation.

- *The kingdom of flowers*
After watching the flights of the surfers, go and enjoy the perfume of the hyacinths
(end of March) or the tulips (up till mid-April), at the Kaandorp and Florimer
establishments just behind the dunes.
Each year, a monumental floral sculpture is made on a precise theme. For the
year 2000 it was Saint-Mark's cathedral in Venice. Each composition requires
half a million to a million hyacinth bells!

Torche Point

MORE INFORMATION?
Association La Torche
Promotion en Plomeur
Place de l'Église, Plomeur
Tel: 02 98 82 09 05
Website: www.latorche.com

*Each spring, to make
the flower bigger,
the "strippers" go into action
with their delicate fingers.*

ty at this time: in the period from 1460 to 1540, in the port registers of the great port of Antwerp, out of 189 Breton boats identified, 121 came from Penmarch! Around 1530, the flotilla was estimated at 300 ships, employing more than 3,000 sailors, ensuring the trade in wines from Bordeaux and the woad plants of Lauragais (Toulouse region), towards Flanders and Holland.

Alas, Penmarch was ravaged in 1595, during the wars of the Leaguers, by the well-known bandit La Fontenelle who massacred hundreds of its inhabitants. The town never really recovered from his terrible crimes.

In Kerity itself, much more than the Saint-Thumette church (a very fine Pietà, certainly from the 15th century), several houses belonging to ship-owners and merchants from the 16th and 17th centuries recall this grandiose epoch.

Saint-Pierre

We are now at Penmarch "Point" and, for ever, the sailors had to be protected from the very dangerous reefs... thus the presence of two lighthouses and a chapel (15th century), a former fire tower.

In 1835 the first oil-lit lighthouse was built, whose power soon turned out to be too weak. These days it is a maritime discovery centre (tel. 02 98 58 72 27).

In 1897, the Eckmül lighthouse was inaugurated, built thanks to the donations of the marchioness of Bloqueville, daughter of Marshal Davout (prince of Eckmül).

Torche Point:
tonic Brittany.

Entry is free, you only have to ... climb the 307 steps to reach the balcony under the lantern. The view from there (at 65 m) is worth the effort.

Saint-Guénolé

The chapel of Notre-Dame-de-la-Joie (15th century) is one of the rare chapels of Cournouaille built on the sea front: it was intended to protect sailors in peril and to house objects saved from shipwrecks.

These days, Saint-Guénolé is a very active port, the sixth in France for fresh fish (crawfish especially). There are also the famous "Rocks", gigantic and christened with evocative names: the "Victims rock", the "Holy Water rock"...

A word of advice: even when the weather seems calm, be very careful; a traitor wave can suddenly surge up, as on October 10th 1870, carrying away five victims including Madame Levainville, wife of the Prefect of Finistère, and her daughter.

 Penmarch

MORE INFORMATION?
Tourist office
Place Davout, BP 47,
29760 Penmarch
Tel.: 02 98 58 81 44 —
Fax: 02 98 58 86 62
E-mail:
otpenmarch@wanadoo. fr

 Eckmül
Lighthouse

MORE INFORMATION?
Phare d'Eckmül
Tel.: 02 98 58 61 17
Do not forget to go and pay homage to the lifeboat "Papa Poydenot", built in 1901 and renovated in 1990-92, classified as a historic monument. It can be seen in its shelter, behind the Eckmül lighthouse.

Saint-Jean-Trolimon: the chapel and calvary of Tronoën

From Torche Point, take a little route winding through the marshes and mounds of the dunes, to find the "cathedral of the dunes": Notre-Dame de Tronoën. It was built in the 15th century on an old sacred site dedicated to Venus, and is open to the light through the apse, with its great stained glass window with rayonnant tracery.

The calvary (1450) is said to be the oldest of the great Breton calvaries and shows nineteen scenes from the life of Christ on two levels of friezes. The Nativity is absolutely exceptional; the hair of the Virgin is wonderfully sculpted, as are the drapes of the bed and pillow. A marvel of finesse!

Plonéour-Lanvern

This vast commune, the most extensive of the Bigouden country, is appreciated most of all for its open natural spaces: 8 km of shore dominated by an immense cordon of smooth stones, and at the foot, pastures and pools spreading out lazily, with thousands of nesting birds (paths and treks and guided excursions).

Amongst the chapels of the commune, Notre-Dame-de-Languivoa is undoubtedly the most impressive (14th to 16th centuries) and its dimensions are surprising. Inside, there is a very beautiful statue of the "Virgin nursing", in polychrome stone (14th), which is admired by everyone. The absence of a belfry is explained by the fact that it was "decapitated" in reprisal for the Red Bonnets revolt (ask for the key at the town hall).

Pouldreuzic

First of all this commune was known for the famous "Henaff pâté" (1907) before the work "The Horse of Pride" extended its reputation across the five continents, soon after it appeared in 1975. Its author, Pierre-Jakez Hélias (1914-1995), born in Pouldreuzic, recounts the life of his ancestors and the traditions of Bigouden country. Over three million copies of the "Horse of Pride", translated into nineteen languages, were sold!

Notre-Dame-de-Languivoa. This polychrome statue, one of the most beautiful in Brittany, is worth the detour.

*The Tronoën Calvary,
one of the oldest in Brittany,
together with that of
Kerbreudeur near Spézet,
is to be read anticlockwise.*

Penhors chapel

Facing Audierne Bay, this is the setting for a pardon, (religious procession), which is one of the most frequented of Bigouden country. As Hélias wrote: *"There is our very own chapel, Notre-Dame de Penhors. Its grand pardon is the summit of our religious life. It is also our great pride because it gathers together such a crowd of strangers here that our Virgin must surely be one of the most powerful amongst the ladies of the land".*

A word of advice: to reach the chapel, take the "beggars' path", bordered by little stone walls, which winds near the Breiz Armor hotel. It recalls the presence of the many who came to the grand pardon of Penhors in former years, to beg for alms.

*The grand Pardon
of Notre-Dame-de-Penhors
takes place in September
and then you can admire
some of the last magnificent
head-dresses from Finistère.*

*The "Human Rights" menhir.
"Here, around this Druids'
stone are buried about
600 drowned men from
the 'Human Rights' ship,
wrecked by the storm
of January 14th 1797..."
The inscription on this
megalith bears witness
to the tragic return of this
ship, part of the Ireland
expedition led by General
Hoche. One of the few
survivors, Major Pipon had
the stone engraved, in 1840.*

Plozévet

At the centre of the Audierne Bay, at the limits of Bigouden country, Plozévet offers very fine walks, along the windy ocean.

From Torche Point to Pors Poulhan, the sea and the wind mingle, fully justifying the words of the author of the "Horse of Pride": *"Our country is famous throughout the world for being one of the most beautiful museums of fresh air existing"...* Open up your lungs!

*Between Torche Point
and Pors-Poulhan, a vast beach of sand
and smooth stones.*

The solar wind route

*This tourist route, whose name is a reference to Pierre-Jakez Hélias and his personage "Wind of the Sun", offers an original way of discovering Audierne Bay.
The circuit relies on the natural and cultural heritage of the bay and proposes thirteen stages, between Penmarch and Plogoff.
On each site, there is a table interpreting and evoking a theme: nature (the wind and the ocean swell), architecture (thatched roofs), history, literature, traditions...*

The Solar wind route

WHERE TO FIND INFORMATION?
Ouest Cornouaille Promotion
Maison du Tourisme, Kermaria, BP 41,
29120 Pont-l'Abbé
Tel.: 02 98 82 30 30 — Fax: 02 98 82 32 18
E-mail: ouest. cornouaille@wanadoo. fr
Website: www. ouest-cornouaille. com
To read: "Bigouden country", collection Icono-
Guides, Pub. Ouest-France. "Bigouden country"
by Daniel Yonnet, photos by Michel Thersiquel,
Pub. Apogée.

The little port of Pors Poulhan marks the border between Bigouden country and Cape Sizun, stated clearly by the sculptor René Quilivic on the base of the statue of his Bigoudène: "Ama echu bro bigouden" (Here ends Bigouden country).

The Bigoudène statue at Pors Poulhan.

THE PARISH CLOSES

*"When I wish to know about men,
I listen to the stones of their city talking."*
Plato.

The philosopher was right: the masterpieces in stone of the Parish closes, which are scattered along the Elorn and on the heights of the Léon, recount the history of men... and such a history! From the 14th to the 17th century, certain parishes of Cornouaille and the Léon enjoyed prosperity without precedent, due for the most part to the cultivation and commerce of flax, exported throughout Europe from the port of Morlaix.

The Renaissance (15th to 16th centuries) was a rich period economically and was also that of ostentation of the Catholic Church faced with the rigour preached by the Protestant Reform. Rivalry between the parishes did the rest... for our greatest pleasure.

What is a Parish close? It is an architectural ensemble comprising the church, the calvary, the ossuary and the cemetery.

It is a sacred spot, situated in the centre of the town, and the close is defined by a surrounding wall with entrances at the four cardinal points, with the main entrance solemnised by a triumphal arch.

It would be a sin of pride to pretend to explain in just a few lines the extraordinary riches of the "closes" described in the following three routes of discovery.

Left page, top:
Parish close of Guimiliau.

Left:
**Lampaul-Guimiliau.
Entombment in
polychrome tufa, by
Antoine Chavagnac (1676).**

Right:
**La Martyre: an enigmatic
caryatid with
expressionless gaze and
legs bound.**

The Landerneau circuit
(55 km — 8 stages)

You are now at the heart of "Kersanton country" (grey granite, easier to work), a material carried by boat as far as Landerneau. As for myself, I fell under the charm of the La Martyre close. Here, around 1460, the first "historiated porch" of the Léon was built: on the two sides of the entry into the church there are carvings of many scenes from the life of Christ and the Virgin (the Annunciation, Visitation, Presentation at the Temple...). The Nativity occupies the centre of the spandrel: Marie is represented on her bed, admirably serene, as is Joseph sitting at her side. An amusing detail (typical of the freedom of expression of the "artists" of the epoch), an angel is playing with a tassel set on the pillow.

La Martyre: The Virgin lying down and nursing; the breast and the Child have been victim to an excess of prudery.

The Landivisiau circuit
(90 km — 10 stages)

Between Saint-Vougay to the north, and Commana to the south, passing via Sizun, Locmélar or Guimiliau, there are marvels all around: such as Lampaul-Guimiliau, whose church celebrates Easter and the Passion of Christ. The altarpieces are exceptional, including that of the Passion (Flemish style), the baptistery with its polychrome wood canopy (1650), the Pietà (17th), the Entombment in white stone from Touraine (1676), the "Rood beam" with its bright colours, representing scenes from the Passion, prodigiously fine works.

The Morlaix circuit
(70 km — 8 stages)

Saint-Thégonnec is the uncontested jewel; according to some, it has the most beautiful close, with its triumphal arch, its calvary (1610), the ossuary-chapel (1676) sheltering an "Entombment" sculpted life-size, the church and its treasure (altarpieces, pulpit...).

A reference book: "Saint-Thégonnec, birth and rebirth of a parish close".

The Landerneau circuit

MORE INFORMATION?
Tourist office du pays de
Landerneau-Daoulas
Pont de Rohan 29800 Landerneau
Tel.: 02 98 85 13 09 —
Fax: 02 98 21 39 27

 The Landivisiau circuit

MORE INFORMATION?
Tourist office des monts
d'Arrée
3, rue de l'Argoat 29450 Sizun
Tel.: 02 98 68 88 40 —
Fax: 02 98 68 86 56

The Morlaix circuit

MORE INFORMATION?
Tourist office du pays de Morlaix
Place des Otages 29600 Morlaix
Tel.: 02 98 62 14 94 —
Fax: 02 98 63 84 87

PLOUGUERNEAU IN THE LAND OF SEAWEED GATHERERS

Plouguerneau, the advance-post between the Aber Wrac'h and the pagan lands, paints a rich palette of Breton landscapes along its 45 kilometres of coastline (sunset at the Kastell-Ac'h Point!) As for its heritage, it would take an encyclopaedia to give details of the history of the chapels, crosses (they number 140!), lighthouses, seaweed ovens... scattered over its territory. But, perhaps, I shall just be able to whet your appetite!

Pont-Krac'h, the "Devil's Bridge"

Located in very pleasant natural surroundings, this is a unique monument of its kind, probably built in the iron-age and restructured in the Middle Ages. Since time immemorial it has served to allow passage across the Aber Wrac'h estuary.

Prad-Paol chapel

Just next to Pont-Krac'h, nestled among the greenery, this little chapel which is so delightful is dedicated to Saint Pol Aurélien, the patron saint of

Kastell-Ac'h Point.
For enthusiasts of fresh
sea air and spray.

Pont-Krac'h or the Devil's Bridge, which can be crossed at low tide.

Right: **The Vierge island lighthouse, built between 1897 and 1902, with its height of 82 metres, is the tallest of this type (made entirely out of granite, "decorated" with 12,500 opaline plaques inside). To visit, board a boat at Kastell-Ac'h Point, absolutely unique!**

the Léon. It is told that he made three sources surge up here, by beating his cane thrice on the ground: the first under the chapel, the second in front of the building, and the third at the side of the path (they still exist).

According to another legend the saint had beheaded a dragon which haunted these places, and its head bounced three times, before the saint Pol Aurélien buried it under the Pont Krac'h cross.

The vale of Traon: the Val chapel and its calvary

In the 16th century this seigniorial chapel was built, belonging to the noble families of Le Moyne de Ranvlouc'h and Kergardiou. Their coats of

Iliz-Coz: a big medieval necropolis (63 tombstones). Here, the engraved stone of the knight Prigent de Coativy, founder of the church, who died in 1384.

arms figure on the calvary, where a Pietà in Kersanton granite can be seen. This is the first calvary of Lower-Brittany to be dated (1511) and signed by the artists who created it, the Italians Conci and Toinas, showing the hammer and the set-square, the emblems of their profession.

The Traon vale is criss-crossed by paths leading to mills, through luxurious vegetation. The Beg ar C'Hastell Point offers a fantastic viewpoint over the Aber Wrac'h estuary.

Lilia

When you arrive at Lilia, don't lose time and go straight to Kastell-Ac'h

Point and its panorama which will take your breath away. In front of you, the small isles which, from east to west, are called: Venan isle, Enez ar Vir, Vierge isle, Enez Valan, Lezhent, Stagadon.

On the Beg er Rest isle opposite, the seaweed ovens are still visible, which are a reminder of this activity which made Plouguerneau the "capital of seaweed gatherers". Even these days, the port of Kervinni receives the "gadget boats" which replaced the horses.

Iliz Koz

The Parish church of Tremenac'h, "Iliz Koz" had a well-known pardon where, they say, pure souls could see three suns rising at dawn. The church disappeared under the sands in the 17th and 18th centuries, victim according to legend of the bad behaviour of three local youngsters: mocking a blind rector, they presented him with a black cat to be baptised... but it started mewing... thus revealing the trickery. The priest then predicted that the three "smart alecs" would lose their sight the following night and that the church would cease to exist... which is what happened.

The ruins of Iliz Koz, unearthed in 1970, have given up their buried secrets, including many tombs of priests and knights.

 Plouguerneau

MORE INFORMATION?
Tourist office
Place de l'Europe 29380
Plouguerneau
Tel.: 02 98 04 70 93
To read: two very complete brochures:
"The heritage path" and "Routes of discovery".

The little port of Camaret at dawn. It name means "the port of the curved dyke". The Rocamadour chapel and the Vauban tower.

CAMARET-SUR-MER

"In Brittany, no one dies, they set sail, they unfurl the sail, they go away, they travel."

These few words from the poet Saint-Pol Roux, who decided to set up his "home for eternity" in Camaret, in 1905, is a marvellous illustration of the destiny of this port, so well known since the Middle Ages.

Between the 15th and 18th centuries, Camaret had to withstand the assaults of the English and Spanish fleets: in 1404 and 1453, the former were repulsed; but on the other hand, the latter occupied a Point (since then called the "Spaniards' Point") in 1594 and the town in 1597. In 1694, there was the battle of Camaret where the Anglo-Dutch suffered an overwhelming defeat.

From the 16th century to the beginning of the 20th century, sardine fishing ensured the prosperity of the city, taken over after that by lobster fishing. In 1988, the leading lobster port of France turned the page on an adventure which can now be read on the wood of the old "Mauritanians" recumbent near the "Sillon" dyke.

Notre-Dame-de-Rocamadour

In 1527, the inhabitants of Camaret decided to build a chapel dedicated to the Virgin, at the end of the Sillon dyke, to be under her protection. It was built on a rock, and took the name of "Notre-Dame Roc Madou" (Notre-Dame of the Rock in the middle of the waters).

When and why did it become "Notre-Dame-de-Rocamadour"? There are several versions: for some, the reason is

Camaret: merchant port and fishing port

The Camaret roadstead has always attracted ships looking for a sure shelter: since 1335, every boat wishing to weigh anchor here has had to pay a tax.

 Camaret

MORE INFORMATION?
Tourist office
15, quai Kléber, BP 16,
29570 Camaret-sur-Mer
Tel.: 02 98 27 93 60 —
Fax: 02 98 27 87 22

The customs officers' path: from Styvel quay to Pen Hir Point

Those who love the wide open spaces will be thrilled by this trek which offers the unique opportunity of passing near the major sites of Camaret. Leaving from the Sillon, from Styvel quay, it leads to the Grand Point and then Toulinguet Point; following the Pen-Hat beach (take care, bathing here is dangerous) and passing the Lagatjar menhirs. It then rejoins Pen Hir Point and its very famous "Tas de Pois", which made such an impression on Saint-Pol Roux that he wrote "Here, I discovered the truth of the world."

Pen-Hir Point and its famous Tas de Pois rocks. The view is grandiose from here, a complete panorama; in good weather it is possible to see Molène and Ouessant islands, Cape Sizun and Saint-Mattieu Point.

"In the grandeur of the bay which opens out from the Pen-Hir cove, I glance at the clouds whose shadow covers the coloured expanse of the sea, like ink".
Yvon Le Men.

poor pronunciation of the Breton language; for others it is a homage to a Quercy pilgrimage sanctuary, honoured by the local fishermen. This chapel is filled with ex-votos, the oldest of which date back to the 19th century.

The Vauban tower

This imposing tower in red pebble-dash is the work of the famous military engineer of the Sun-King, who had it built in 1687 to finalise the protection of the grand port of Brest. Several times, Vauban used Camaret as his command post. He distinguished himself, in particular, on June 18th 1694, during the battle against the Anglo-Dutch fleet. The evening of the victory, he was praised and escorted by the whole population.

These days the Vauban tower holds a marine museum focused on local history.

The manor of Coecilian and Saint-Pol Roux

His real name was Paul Roux, and he was born in Marseilles in 1861, before becoming "Saint-Pol Roux" later, in the kingdom of letters. He was conquered by Camaret when he first visited it in 1892, and settled there finally in 1905, on the heights, in his Boultous manor, re-named "de Coecilian" in homage to his son who was killed in the war in 1915.

He hosted many personalities here, from the artistic and political world: André Breton, Max Jacob, Jean Moulin...

Drama struck in June 1940: a German soldier entered the manor, killing Rose, his faithful servant, and wounding the poet and his daughter. Shortly after that the place was pillaged, and the manuscripts burnt or torn up. The ordeal was too much for Saint-Pol Roux, who died on October 18th.

The manor was bombarded by the Allies in 1944... and the ruins were never rebuilt.

Morbihan
a gentle way of life

THE HIDDEN TREASURES OF THE BLAVET VALLEY: FROM PONTIVY TO HENNEBONT

Very close to the over-peopled ocean beaches, there is an oasis of peace, which I have assiduously visited for nearly thirty years; the Blavet river valley. Here you have 50 km of complete tranquillity, along the towpath, only taken by a few cyclists or walkers.

The Blavet, which was canalised in the 19th century, flows peacefully through its wooded meanders, a link between two medieval cities with a rich past; Pontivy and Hennebont. This walk in inner Brittany, between sea and land, reveals very attractive landscapes and a no less attractive heritage.

Pontivy

The town of Pontivy, not to differ from the common rule of so many Breton towns, owes its foundation to a Celt monk, Ivy, who left like so many

Opposite: **Last stage for a little lobster boat at the far end of the Gulf of Morbihan, at the Passage en Saint-Armel.**

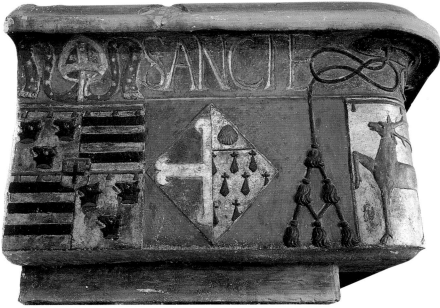

The Rohan castle at Pontivy. A detail of one of the two monumental chimneys showing the mysterious red deer, lifting its hoof proudly.

81

of his fellows to evangelise the "barbarians" of Letavia (as the present Brittany was then called) at the end of the 7th century.

The town offers two totally different aspects, one medieval and the other Napoleonic.

The medieval town

It is marked first of all by its castle, a fine example of the military architecture of the end of the Middle Ages.

This imposing square fortress, with its massive walls 5 metres thick, is due to Jean II, viscount of Rohan, who built it at the end of the 15th century (1479-1485). Despite all the transformations and additions of the following centuries, it still offers visitors a harmonious ensemble, whose internal facades from the 17th and 18th centuries emphasise the residential function for which it was used at this epoch.

How pleasant it is to wander along the old alleys of this historic city on a Monday morning, market day. Here, Bouffay Square.

Pontivy and the powerful Rohan lords

For over a thousand years, the Rohan family was one of the great Breton families. After founding Josselin, the lords of Rohan received from those of Porhoët a castle built at Pontivy, in the 11th century, bearing the name of "Salles".

This was taken and ruined in 1342, by the count of Northampton, from the Monfort side, since viscount Alain VII of Rohan had chosen the opposite camp, that of the Blois-Penthièvre. This was in the middle of the war of Succession in the duchy of Brittany, in which the Rohan family played a very active role. In 1396 they decided to make Pontivy the capital of their viscounty, which became a duchy in 1603.

These powerful lords, rivals of the dukes of Brittany, developed a very active mecenat during the 15th and 16th centuries (art being at the service of politics then), and Pontivy and its region reaped the main benefits: buildings for the castle, of course, but above all numerous chapels with inestimable art treasures.

After the castle, go to the old heart of the city, which has narrow streets bordered by wood framed houses.

The rue du Pont (Bridge street)

This is the main street of the old town and No. 14 is a very fine Renaissance town house, built in 1577, which belonged to the Seneschal of Rohan viscounty.

Martray Square (Market)

In the Middle Ages, on Mondays and Thursdays, there were stalls with fruits and vegetables on sale as well as other products from the rich countryside around.

At the corner of General-de-Gaulle street, note the very elegant Renaissance style pavilion, built in 1578 by the Roscouët family.

The rue du Fil (Thread Street)

This owes its name to the trade in fabric, which contributed greatly to the prosperity of the town up till the 18th century.

The Notre-Dame-de-Joie Basilica

This edifice, with its Flamboyant style decoration, was originally dedicated to Saint Ivy, when it was built in

1532 by Claude de Rohan (fourth son of Jean II), bishop of Quimper. Only at the end of the 17th century, after a terrible epidemic of dysentery, was it placed under the protection of the Virgin.

"Napoléonville"

It extends from Aristide-Briand square (formerly "Napoleon Square") to Marengo Street, through a succession of roads and wide avenues, built in a disciplined fashion, in contrast to the joyous "anarchy" of the medieval quarter.

It owes its arrangement to the express will of the First Consul, Napoleon Bonaparte, to build in the middle of Brittany a town outpost for controlling (that is repressing) the (Royalist) Chouannerie. We are in 1802, September 17th to be precise, when he ordered the canalisation of the river Blavet... and the construction of a huge barracks for his troops.

The reason was that since 1793, the Chouans of Brittany regularly attacked the authorities of the Republic, and

One of the best preserved castles in Brittany with its military architecture from the end of the Middle Ages. A decor worthy of an epic film.

Pontivy and Napoleon

Created by Napoleon I, "Napoléonville" was renamed Pontivy in 1815... before returning to this name again in 1852 under Napoleon III. He made a notable visit in 1858, during which he promised to build a church in this new quarter of the town. Thus, the Saint-Joseph church saw the light of day (with its splendid stained glass windows by contemporary artists).

In 1870, with the fall of Napoleon III, Napoléonville lost its name again and the National Assembly gave it back its original name: Pontivy.

The altarpiece in the Houssaye chapel (detail), one of the marvels of Rohan country.

Pontivy: detail from the front door of a house, end of the 19th century.

then the Consulate. Shortly after taking power, in November 1799 (after a coup d'état), Bonaparte had to call in the army of General Brune to put an end to the ambitions of the General-in Chief of the Chouans, Georges Cadoudal.

The peace treaty, signed at the Château de Beauregard, near Vannes, in February 1800, turned out to be fairly fragile; one had to be vigilant faced with these turbulent Bretons!

On May 10th 1805, in Milan, Napoleon I decreed the construction of a new town, to the south of Pontivy, and the name had to be changed to "Napoléonville". The project was given to the engineer Chabrol. The fall of the Empire in 1814 marked the end of most of the works.

"Napoléonville" can be visited around the big square called "la Plaine": the town hall, the sub-prefecture, the palace of justice and the Saint-Joseph church, which still bear witness to this "glorious" past.

After "Napoléonville" turn towards the chapel of Notre-Dame de la Houssaye, one of the jewels of religious art in the Rohan lands. Again it was viscount Jean II de Rohan who ordered the construction of this magnificent edifice: the "signature" of the Rohan family (the heraldic 'mascles', or lozenges voided) is clearly apparent in the choir window.

The altarpiece of the main altar (without doubt created by a workshop in Amiens, at the beginning of the 16th century) is a pure masterpiece of sculpture: 102 figures illustrate, in thirteen settings, various scenes from the Passion of Christ, with the Crucifixion occupying the central place.

The quality of the work, the expression of the faces leave you breathless... as well as certain "savoury" details: one of the soldiers sticking out his tongue; Simon the Cyrenian losing his breeches.

Saint-Nicolas-des-Eaux

At the foot of the Castennec "mountain", this hamlet, bathed by the peaceful waters of the river Blavet, is one of

Pontivy

MORE INFORMATION?

Tourist office
61, rue du Général-de-Gaulle 56300 Pontivy
Tel.: 02 97 25 24 10
Rohan tourist country
2, place Bisson
56303 Pontivy Cedex
Tel.: 02 97 25 01 70

The splendour of the chapels of Rohan country

Few regions possess as many marvels of religious art: Noyal-Pontivy (Sainte-Noyale), Neuillac (Notre-Dame-de-Carmes), Saint-Thuriau (parish church) etc.

Nonetheless may I pick out the Saint-Mériadec chapel in Stival: its 15th century stained glass windows and its wall paintings (beginning of the 16th century) are well worth the visit. The latter paintings show the life of Saint Mériadec in twelve scenes... and the Rohan family claims to be his descendants!

In particular, note: the "Saint Mériadec bonnet", a bell which the saint rang above the deaf, to cure them of their infirmity immediately.

The Saint-Gildas chapel, takes a special place in Brittany's heritage. It is one of the stops for the exhibition of contemporary art held each summer: Art in the chapels.

beams in the 16th century church) to reach the Crano heaths, the realm of the "kourils" and other goblins.

Saint-Gildas chapel

The chapel is sheltered by an enormous rock, and has been built around its granite wall. Instead of using the term "chapel", it would be more appropriate to call it a "hermitage" since it owes its reputation to Saint Gildas who retreated to this place to live in prayer and solitude, after founding a monastery on the Rhuys peninsula (6th century).

Although the interior of the building is not very interesting (it was restored in 1837), there is a "sounding stone" which is still fascinating these days. If you strike it with another stone you will hear a strange sound, like the noise of an anvil.

Saint-Nicodème chapel

This chapel, perched on the heights overlooking the valley is, without the most popular tourist sites of the valley. There are boat trips, walks or cycling routes; everything invites you to take time to relax.

The towpath

As far as the Rimaison mill (direction Pontivy): this is a very pleasant walk, which takes you to this final vestige (with its finely sculpted Renaissance facade) of the lords whose authority extended in earlier days over the whole of the land.

The Castennec circuit (12 km on foot)

Leave from the small town of Bieuzy-les-Eaux (stained glass windows and

Art in the chapels

This is an original initiative to be applauded: why not try to establish a dialogue between the language of contemporary art and that of past centuries? This delicate task, undertaken by the association called "Art in the Chapels", has been crowned with success: thousands of visitors come each year to admire the works of known artists (Geneviève Asse in 1999, Gérard Titus-Carmel in 2000, etc.), placed carefully in an intimate framework.

contest, one of the most beautiful in Brittany. Note the belfry rising up to 50 m high, the altarpiece in white stone with its Descent from the Cross, and the great fountain with three pools.

The former presbytery, attached to this building, now houses the association called Art in the Chapels.

 L'art dans les chapelles

MORE INFORMATION?
Association L'Art dans les chapelles
Presbytère de
Saint-Nicodème
56930 Pluméliau
Tel.: 02 97 51 97 21
Website:
www. art chapelles. com

Above: **Saint-Nicodème chapel, its bell-tower emerging from the fields, is unique in Brittany.**

The towpath along the river: an oasis of peace, pure happiness.

The Cartopole at Baud

This regional conservatory of postcards, opened in 1996, is a unique collection of its type, offering visitors and researchers the possibility of plunging into the heart of Brittany of previous years, those of 1900-1920, the golden age of the postcard.

What pleasure it is to discover here the activities of yesteryear: the beating of rye, the harvest of Roscoff onions (then sold to the "Johnnies" in England)... and the other trades: horse traders, money lenders, tooth-drawers, stone breakers, mole catchers, wooden spoon salesmen.

*The restored village of Poul Fetan is alive and well.
In good weather,
you can wash your clothes
in the company of charming laundresses.*

2639. – La Boutique du Marchand de Cheveux

 Cartopole

MORE INFORMATION?
Cartopole
Rue d'Auray 56150 Baud
Tel.: 02 97 51 15 14 —
Fax: 02 97 39 02 39
Internet :
www. cartopole. org.

Quistinic and the village of Poul Fetan

I have very special tender feelings for this commune and its inhabitants. In fact, at the beginning of the sixties, the fashion was all "re-allocation of land" (remembrement)... and the bulldozers came in wickedly to destroy the banks carefully built up over the preceding centuries. Quistinic managed to resist the song of the sirens of so-called "progress", and the result can be seen elsewhere now: since the rainwater is not held back, it runs quickly into the Brittany water courses carrying the nitrates accumulated on the fields... "Bonjour", green tides!

"Poul": wash-house; "Fetan": source.

Poul Fetan, which was reduced to a few ruined farms thirty years ago, is now one of the main tourist sites of the Morbihan. What a revenge for a fate which seemed to be inevitable at first sight: just like so many Breton villages victim of "rural abandon", it seemed doomed to disappear... but the determined will and endless efforts of the inhabitants of Quistinic gave it new life, and what a life!

Among the farmhouses of the 17th and 18th centuries, superbly restored, affable girls dressed in the farming costumes of the epoch repeat the gestures of peasant life: milking cows, producing butter, spinning wool... and you can take part in all these activities yourself, just as you can "lend a

hand" to knead the dough for the bread, etc.

The wash day in the wash-house does not even forget the gossip which took place there

Poul Fetan offers activities all year round, as well as its Fair of Yesteryear on August 15th and its Cider Fair on the fourth Sunday of September.

And something else not to be forgotten: take the time to stroll along the paths bordered by little dry-stone walls, between waterfalls and perfumed heaths, revealing the magnificent viewpoints over the Blavet valley.

Poul Fetan, a timeless village!

Hennebont

Pontivy — Hennebont: from one medieval city to another... and a common origin, a bridge, "Hen pont", or "Bridge road" (or the "old bridge" according to another version).

Hennebont no longer holds any traces of the castle of the powerful

The Venus of Quinipily

This statue, of enigmatic origin, has aroused curiosity for centuries: the "Venus" standing on a base, in the enclosure of the ruins of Quinipily castle, when leaving Baud. Its story is worth writing down. Formerly, it enthroned the Castennec mountain, where the inhabitants believed it had fertility powers. And so, many local women came to pay homage to the "gwreg houarn" (the iron lady), also called "groah ar Goard" (the Coarde lady), from the name of the neighbouring farm. They bathed (naked?) in the water trough at the foot of the statue... to the anger of the church priest who complained to the local lord of the manor, count Claude II of Lannion. In 1661, he ordered that it should be thrown into the river... but in 1664, the inhabitants lifted it out and put it back into place... to continue their "non-Catholic" rites. It was thrown into the river a second time, under the instructions of the bishop of Vannes. But in 1696, Pierre de Lannion, who had just succeeded his father, had it taken out of the river Blavet and carried to his Quinipily castle.

lords of Kemenet-Heboé, built in the feudal epoch (11th to 13th centuries), but it compensates fully for this "lack" because of the ramparts and its fortified town, concrete evidence of a prestigious medieval past.

Hennebont ramparts with gardens à la française.

The Siege of Hennebont.
Froissart Chronicle.
14th century.
National Library, Paris.

The fortified town and its ramparts

Enter the town through the Broërec gateway. It is flanked by two massive granite towers, and houses a little museum of history, art and local traditions. This is the ultimate vestige of the fortifications built around 1260, at the order of Jean Le Roux, Duke of Brittany.

Hennebont, a medieval city at the end of the Blavet estuary, developed considerably between the 11th and 13th centuries, and became a well-known stronghold... and thus a strategic point during the Breton war of Succession, which opposed two strong sides: the Montforts and the Blois-Penthièvre.

In 1342, Jeanne de Flandres, wide of Jean de Montfort, took refuge here, when she was attacked by the troops of Charles de Blois. She was cunning and courageous, and went out one night with her garrison to set fire to the enemy camp. Since then she has been called "Jeanne la Flamme". Between 1364 and 1373, the town was occupied by the English, before being freed by the famous High Constable of France, Bertrand du Guesclin.

You can re-live this atmosphere of sieges and deadly attacks here, on the ramparts, which were strengthened in the 15th century, under Jean V Duke of Brittany.

In September, the grand Pardon of Notre-Dame-du-Vœu. An inhabitant proudly wearing the Lorient head-dress, nicknamed the "aeroplane".

The Notre-Dame-de-Paradis Basilica

The best view over the Basilica is from the present Maréchal-Foch square (formerly Paradise square), which is bordered by interesting buildings from the 16th century (the tourist office), the 17th century (the Vieux Logis bar and the former town house of the Coëssin de la Berraye family), and the 18th century (decorated façade of the town hall).

Inside the Basilica, the Renaissance gallery houses one of the oldest organs of Morbihan (1652) and the contemporary stained glass windows (by the artist Max Ingrand) which recount the history of the town, including the famous "Vow" made in 1699. At that time a terrible epidemic of the plague ravaged the region, and the inhabitants of Hennebont asked the Virgin to protect them, and "vowed" to her... the miracle took place and they were spared. On the last Sunday of September each year, there is a pardon, in celebration of this Vow.

G. Bourgain ℰt
à monsieur Roussin
La seule esquisse de mes dessins, qui me reste

Attack of the Chouans.
G. Bourgain, tinted drawing.
Municipal Library,
Fougères

IN THE TRACKS OF THE CHOUANS IN AURAY COUNTRY

"Chouans!"

This word resounds loud and strong, just like the Breton peasants' uprising (1793-1800), in which Georges Cadoudal played a major role. Luckily,

Auray and the surrounding communes have kept many traces of this troubled epoch: country paths, chapels, crosses... perpetuating the memory of these "Chouans", who have been given an unflattering portrait in the history books. They are too often depicted as individuals with wild-looking expressions, fighting to the death for the white flag (that is, the Royalist flag, after the French Revolution).

Reality should be more flexible: although they supported the ideals of justice and equality set forward by the 1789 Revolution, the "farm labourers" of Brittany (like those of Vendée) felt that they had been betrayed by the bourgeoisie in power, between 1789 and 1793. That very year, on March 19th, a young man 22 years old brandished the flag of the revolt, during the battle of Mane Corohan, at the gates of Auray. His name was Georges Cadoudal.

Georges Cadoudal (1771-1804)

Georges Cadoudal was born on January 1st 1771, in the village of Kerleano, in the parish of Brec'h, into a family of rich farmers. In 1789, when he was a pupil at the Saint-Yves college in Vannes, he enthusiastically supported the youth of the Commonality de Rennes opposed to those of the nobility ("Days of Bricoles", January 26-27th).

He was saddened and then disgusted by these bourgeois who confiscated all the powers (political and economic), and joined the Counter-Revolutionary camp. After distinguishing himself in the Vendée wars (June to December 1793), he headed the Chouans of the Auray lands. He demonstrated unusual qualities as strategist and leader of men, during the "Emigrés expedition to Quiberon" and in 1795, on August 16th, he was promoted to "General" of the Morbihan Chouans.

He was a resolute opponent of the Republican General Hoche, and Napoleon Bonaparte the First Consul then, and was guillotined in Paris on June 25th 1804.

Portrait of Georges Cadoudal by Aimable Paul Coutan. Museum of Art and History of Cholet.
Photo Studio Golder, Cholet.

Locoal-Mendon: the "Cadoudal path"

The path of this portion of history - and legend - starts from the Point of the Forest peninsula (in Locoal, follow the "route des Chouans" panels).

92

Straight away, enormous hundred-year old oaks invite you to plunge into the heart of this land of woods and pastures, where the Chouan-peasants could move around so easily. The high

banks bordering the narrow paths fully justified the strategy set out by Cadoudal: surprise the Blue (Republican) patrols, take their weapons immediately, and disappear just as quickly.

On the way, admire the superb glimpses of the Étel ria, and you will find yourselves in the "Cadoudal hideout", lost among the oaks and foliage. Continue the walk, so calm these days, until you reach the Point "de Beg er Lannec" where previously, there were boats waiting to carry Cadoudal and his chiefs of staff, in the case of danger. As his biography states: *"One day, despite the treaties, three Republican detachments arrived at Locoal to try to encircle his hideout. Georges, who saw them and was seen by them, left by sea with his chiefs of staff under their very*

The Chouan treasure, in the Forest

"Kadoudal has the custom of depositing his money in the little isle of Loquale near Mendon, in the L'Afforêt village at the end of the isle, with the priest of this place, named L'Auneau, brother of the parish priest of this commune: there are considerable deposits here, where Georges Kadoudal sometimes retreats..."

These revelations were made by Kobbé, one of the lieutenants of "general" Georges, when he was arrested by the "Blues". They confirm that there considerable transfers of funds in this Forest hamlet, where Cadoudal had set up his headquarters. The memory of this money, intended to finance the "Chouannerie" is perpetuated in a local legend:

« En ur park tri-horneg	In a triangular field
Ema eur er chouaned	You will find the Chouan gold
Er bazenn e so en héol »	The stone is in the sun.

The treasure... if it exists... has never been found!

noses, leaving behind him those who had flattered themselves that he could not escape them..."

Ploemel: the village of Saint-Laurent

It is so wonderful to discover this village with its fine granite dwellings, whose venerable walls are still haunted by the memory of Father Lomenec'h! He was a non-juring priest, the confidant and... secret agent of Georges Cadoudal, who often took refuge in this hamlet.

Moreover, in this chapel, with its typical Flamboyant Gothic porch, he celebrated mass and gave the sacrament. When there was danger, there were deep country paths enabling him to flee to Keraveon castle or the Saint-Cado

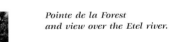

It is not surprising that the Chouans lost the battle if all the "Blues" looked like this!

Pointe de la Forest and view over the Etel river.

93

Auray

MORE INFORMATION?
Tourist office
20, rue du Lait
56400 Auray
Tel.: 02 97 24 09 75
Useful reading:
"The Chouan route in
Auray country", topo-guide
where 23 stages of this
historic, and touristic route
are given in detail

chapel... which these days you can also reach through very pleasant walks.

Brec'h: the Martyrs' field

When the Royalists surrendered, at Fort-Neuf in Quiberon, on July 21st 1795, the prisoners had to march as far as Auray, where they were literally squashed into the prison and the religious buildings. They were then judged by military commissions, and 748 were executed in Vannes, Brec'h and the Quiberon peninsula.

Here, later named the "Martyrs' field", 206 Chouans and émigrés were shot. In 1814; their remains were transferred to the Chartreuse chapel close by.

Auray

The cells of the former royal prison

Within these walls of the present History House you can visit the gaols of the "Old Régime": the enormous doors in solid oak, the side walls covered with graffiti bearing the names and the dates (1801, 1821, 1830...) bearing witness to the terrible universe of imprisonment of that time.

Georges Cadoudal was imprisoned here for the first time in 1793, before returning the following year with his whole family. In 1795, many Royalist officers, made prisoner at Quiberon, lived here in execrable conditions, before being judged.

The Kerleano village and mausoleum

A majestic alley leads to the village of his birth... the last dwelling of the "commander in chief of the Royal and Catholic Army of Brittany", Georges Cadoudal.

These days he rests in the central well of an imposing mausoleum, built in the 19th century, together with his faithful lieutenant and friend, Mercier "la Vendée". After this, many members of the Cadoudal family (ennobled under the Restoration) were buried in this monument.

Saint-Laurent Chapel at Ploemel.

THE GULF OF MORBIHAN

"When the sacrilegious axe of man began to profane the secular forest of Rhuys, the fairies, whose mysterious caves can still be found, decided to leave these inhospitable places. They flew away like a swarm towards the thick inland forests. While they were crossing Morbihan, gold dust fell from their cloaks... and isles rose up everywhere, as numerous as the days of the year."

The legend thus delivers the secret of the birth of this Gulf of Morbihan ("little sea"), whose banks and isles are pure enchantment. But how many isles are there, really? Some say 365, others say 42, but does it really matter! The Gulf of Morbihan is the refuge of so many nature lovers, and a small paradise to discover peacefully. Let us open the door at Kerpenhir Point; we shall close it at that of Port-Navalo.

Locmariaquer

If there exists a place "blessed by the gods"... and cherished by man, it is certainly this commune: the populations of the Neolithic age discovered here a welcoming haven (and no doubt made it a sacred site), as the megaliths attest; the Romans built a very active city here, as proved by many remains discovered in the 19th century, to such an extent that some archaeologists claimed that this must have been Darioritum, capital of the Veneti... to the great anger of Vannes which has always claimed this honour.

This antique town, secret and quiet, only reveals its beauty to those who are not in a hurry, those who arrive here by the footpath, which leads from the "Great Broken Menhir" to rejoin the site majestically afterwards.

An impressive view of the Gulf of Morbihan, from Locmariaquer. Blair Point can be seen at the mouth of the river Auray.

The statue of Notre-Dame-de-Kerdro watches over the entrance to the Gulf of Morbihan at Kerpenhir Point, opposite the Rhys peninsula and Port-Navalo.

The statue of Notre-Dame-de-Kerdro

This statue, erected in 1962, replaces the one set in place in the 19th century, knocked down by the Germans in 1940. It is witness of the protection for sailors, for a safe return, provided by "Notre-Dame-du-Bon-Voyage... and du-Bon-Retour". Many sailors' wives have come here to ask her to intercede on behalf of their husbands.

Kerpenhir Point

High up on the black rocks, the statue of Notre-Dame-de-Kerdro keeps a vigilant watch over the mouth of the Morbihan Gulf. In fact, there are very fast currents here: when the tide rises, the water from the ocean rushes into the narrow neck, and is called the "Mare's cur-

A site unique in the world, at Locmariaquer, grouping the Merchants' Table, the Great Broken Menhir and the Ergrah tumulus.

rent", tipping the waves with spray; then when the tide starts ebbing, the waves rush back, sometimes boiling so much that they have been called the "Witches' cauldron".

When winds and currents are in opposite directions, you can even hear the moaning of the "Port-Navalo groaner", and there are choppy seas which are the terror of small boats. And woe to those who take no notice: how many yachts, which ignored the warning of the "groaner", have been smashed onto the rocks!

Larmor-Baden

This is a young commune (it only separated from Baden in 1924), and offers all the charms of the gulf, from the double aspect of nature and history.

Kerpenhir Point and a general view of Locmariaquer.

1984: a sensational archaeological discovery

The Gavrinis cairn was discovered in 1832, and the first excavations started in 1835. They were re-started in 1969, and considerably changed the understanding about this monument.

In 1984, archaeologists decided to free the hidden face of the stone slabs, revealing engravings which seemed to come from even older megaliths. The most astonishing turned out to be the flat slab covering the chamber: its upper face carries a big axe-plough, a bovine outline and the horns and neck of a second animal.

But this slab links with two others, one of them forming the cover of the "Merchants' Table", and the other that of the "Er Vinglé" cave...located in Locmariaquer! The surprise was enormous. Charles-Tanguy Leroux, the archaeologist in charge of the excavation demonstrated perfectly (by studying the cracks and the designs) that these three stones had originally formed a menhir 14 metres high, no doubt standing not far from the "Great Broken Menhir". It had been broken up into three pieces and moved to cover the three tombs. Archaeology sometimes reveals surprising discoveries.

Enter the dimly lit corridor in the Gavrinis cairn, and go back 5,000 years in time. An unforgettable visit.

The Pen An Toul marshes

These ancient salt marshes are now the refuge of many species of birds which come in to feed, to rest and to reproduce: the white-headed stilt, the common tern, the ringed plover, the redshank, the red-billed shelduck, etc.

There is a footpath for walking all round and observing. But do not make any noise... and do not forget your binoculars!

Locmiquel, Berchis and Pen Lannic Points

Please forget your car, for once: you must explore the many paths or trails on foot or by bicycle. From here, you can contemplate ever-changing nuptials of the sky, the earth and the sea.

Pen Lannic is a small peaceful port, from where one can board for cruises in the Gulf... and to the very mysterious Gavrinis island.

Gavrinis Island

After a crossing of barely fifteen minutes, you will land on this isle which is known throughout the world for its megalith listed as a "masterpiece of universal art": the Gavrinis cairn. Its dimensions are impressive (50 metres in diameter and 6 metres high), and it covers a big dolmen whose corridor, 14 metres long, ends in a simple chamber, located practically at the centre of the cairn.

It was probably intended for the cult of the dead, and has a classic form, which was very often built in Brittany, between 4500 and 3000 B.C. But its exceptional decoration is much less common: twenty-three pillars decorated with sculptures in which curved lines of granite design spirals, circles, semicircles, in a mad saraband dance where several known symbols of megalithic art are to be found: snakes, axes, bows and arrows, crosses, figures in "escutcheons" (identifiable as human beings?) etc.

Astonishment and admiration becomes even greater when you realise that these Neolithic artists made these sculptures with the aid of quartz strikers, the only material able to attack the granite, which is a very hard material to work.

The tour of the Gulf, by boat

If there is one excursion to be made by boat in Brittany, then it is the "Tour of the Gulf", which is offered by several companies leaving from Locmariaquer, Port-Blanc (in Baden), Vannes, Port-Navalo etc.
During the cruise you will discover the islands of Gavrinis and Er Lannic, the little islets of Boédé and Boëdic, formerly frequented by proud sinagots (old sailing boats with a shallow hull), Hur, Huric, Godec... They are all jewels in the crown of this gulf, but the "pearl" is the Monks' Island (Île aux Moines), to be seen on the horizon... and next Arz Island, from the bow of the boat
I myself have a very clear memory of a cruise taken in the month of June, accompanied by a fine dinner, under a sunset which really was...dazzling.

This agricultural vocation, well established in the Middle Ages, has given way to the flood of tourists impatient to march along the little routes and perfumed footpaths of the isle of flowers. You will become heady with the sweet scents, as soon as you come to the first fishermen's houses leading to the centre of the small town. Depending on the season, the gardens are filled with the

Berder Island.
To be reached, on foot... at low tide (be careful to consult the time of the tides). There is a path all around this wooded isle, which provides magnificent views of its neighbours: Gavrinis, île aux Moines, île de la Jument... Facing the latter, at the south of Berder, you can spend time watching the ships and yachts racing along the famous "Jument current" or desperately struggling... against the current.

The Ile aux Moines

The first trace of its owners can be found in the very old cartulary in Redon: *"Dedit Erispoe... insulam quoe vocature Crialeis, id est enes manac, ad fabas, monachis sanctis Salvatoris."* This text tells us that, around 854, the king of Brittany, Erispoe, donated the isle called "Crialeis" to the monks of the Saint-Sauveur abbey of Redon...to cultivate broad beans and haricot beans.

subtle shades of camellia, wisteria and mimosa, rhododendrons, hydrangeas, magnolias: a real symphony of colours.

The Wood of Amour (Love), Wood of Soupirs (Sighs) and Wood of Regrets bring a deliciously romantic note to the country picture of this isle which is so calm: there are hardly any cars, motorbikes or other backfiring engines here; the place is for walkers... and dreamers. From Port-Miquel, the coastal path takes you to the grandiose panoramas of Trech Point, with an unequalled view over the isles of Irus, Olavre and Arz... Two other walks are suggested, to Brouel Point (passing via Guerric cove bordered by hundred-year old oak trees) and to Pen Hap Point.

House with its flowers on the Ile aux Moines.

The Ile d'Arz

You board at Conleau Point, a short walk from the centre of Vannes, for a very pleasant little trip, before reaching the shore at Béhuré. And here you are, on Arz Island "the captains' island". The origin of the name can be found in the cemetery next to the Parish church: there is an astonishing number of tombstones marking the graves of

The Ile aux Moines: the longest island in the Gulf (3 1/2 miles). In the foreground, Pen-Hap Point.

Waiting for the tide, Arz island.

99

The legend of the lovers of Arz and Izenah

In those days, the islands of Arz and Izenah were only one, linked together by a narrow causeway at Brouël Point. And each day created by God, a young island girl walked along this causeway to meet an Ildarais with whom she was deeply in love. I must tell you that there was a custom then, completely unusual, that allowed the girls of the islands to ask the young men for their hand in marriage. But alas! The beauty was the only daughter of a rich sea captain, "seignior of the seas", while the young man was the son of a simple fisherman. The "fiancé" was soon forced to enter the monastery in Arz and to take his vows. So, did the proud island lass give up her love? This doesn't take into account the Breton obstinacy... and each evening the sweet girl took the causeway to find her beloved.

The prior was furious and called on divine intervention to stop such "diabolic" love. Thus, one evening when the beauty was walking along the narrow pathway, enormous waves suddenly rose up and carried her away into the depths, and since this time the two islands have always been apart.

former captains or commanders of merchant vessels and ships of the Royal Navy.

Since, from their early days, the sailors from Arz understood the currents of the gulf, their (justified) reputation opened the way for them to be given command positions.

After visiting the Notre-Dame church, whose origins go back to the 11th century, set off (on foot, of course!) along the little routes and paths leading to Bilhervé Point, or Liouse or Berno Points. The tidal mill on the Berno dyke has recently been restored and is well worth visiting. It operated from the 17th century to the beginning of the 20th, but was then a victim of "progress" and would certainly have fallen completely into ruin if Jean Bulot (former commander of the "Abeille", a deep sea tugboat) had not decided to face the challenge. The rebirth of this tidal mill of Berno is certainly the best homage any "Ildarais" could

Regattas of old riggings during the Red-Sails fête at Séné. Here, the "Jean-et-Jeanne" sinagot.

Left: **Shelduck** *photo E. Barbelette*
Centre: **Little egret.**
Right: **: Cabot's tern**. *photo J.-L. Le Moigne*

pay to his compatriots who, moreover deserve warm congratulations for being able to preserve their island from all the ugliness which much too often disfigures the coasts. There are no big buildings, nothing but nature, friendly and inviting.

Séné

The inhabitants of this little town, situated a few hundred metres from Vannes, are called "Sinagots"... just like the famous fishing boats with their black hulls and red sails. They are perfectly adapted to the shallow depths and subtle currents, and brought prosperity to the sailors of Séné in the 19th and 20th centuries, before giving way to bigger crafts. We must be grateful to the rebirth of the maritime heritage, which allows us once again to see these proud and colourful sailing boats.

Séné, with its wealth of sinagots, reserves unexpected treasures for "enlightened" ramblers: the old tidal

The birds of the Gulf of Morbihan

The gulf shelters one of the most extraordinary concentrations of birds: about 100,000, with 110 duly documented species.
Marshes and silts provide abundant food and here you can see the egret *chasing prawns, the* shelduck *swallowing worms and shellfish... all year round there are varied species here, such as auks and guillemots,* terns *and* stilts... *From November to February, tens of thousands of migrating birds come here to rest: on their way from Lapland to Africa,* spotted redshanks *and* greenshanks *stop a while here. But above all, the* Brent geese *(and their famous "cackling") have chosen the gulf as their favourite refuge. The marshes between Falguérec and Séné, between Duer and Sarzeau, and those of Pen An Toul, in Larmor-Baden, are all very special observation posts.*

The Falguérec reserve

This vast humid zone - 550 acres of old salt marshes - is a very frequented stopping place for many species of migrating birds. Among others, the black-winged stilt *and the* pied avocet *nest here...*
A path has been made leading to observation posts in wood, and you can watch the birds from here, without disturbing them. Regular visits are organised, under the direction of nature guides, who are the only ones able to explain in detail the life of these protected species.

 The Falguérec reserve

WHERE TO FIND INFORMATION?
Nature Reserve of the Séné marshes
Tel.: 02 97 66 92 76

mill of Cantizac, the sculpted cross of Montsarrac, and superb views over the gulf to the Layle and Port-Anna peninsulas and Bil and Montsarrac Points.

Saint-Armel

This commune, turned towards the gulf, has (for the moment) escaped the wave of tourists arriving on the Rhuys peninsula since the sixties.

In the Middle Ages, Saint-Armel was only a village, created in the 11th century by the monks from the abbey of Saint-Gildas-de-Rhuys. They were also the founders of the villages of Lasné, Le Passage, La Villeneuve and l'ile Tascon. They developed the salt marshes, which were exploited until the 20th century. Saint-Armel has several interesting sites... and a bakery whose fame goes far beyond the limits of the village. Here the baker will prepare one of the local specialities for you, such as the "Gochtial", a sort of milk bread, which will catch you, without remorse, in the sin of gluttony!

Le Passage

This peaceful village owes its name to a very old tradition, confirmed by a charter signed on March 8th, 1367, by Jean IV Duke of Brittany, ensuring rights of passage, *"wherever you go between Rhuys and Vannes"*. It was given in return for coins of the realm: *"gentle-ladies"* and *"villains"* could thus cross the fairway on the ferry,

accompanied by their cattle (oxen and horses).

These days, Saint-Armel and Le Passage invite you to discover the nooks and corners of the gulf, with a network of marked paths. And then, just going off a path, stop at an oyster farm and taste the delicious oysters of the peninsula.

The Lasné marshes

Salt, omnipresent in the Rhuys peninsula, formed the landscapes of the Lasné marshes: in the 15th century, François II, Duke of Brittany, conceded "several dunes and salt marshes" to his Secretary Jean

Quistinic isle, facing
Le Passage en Saint-Armel.

Maubec (owner of the Manor of Truscat), to be converted into salt pans. During the following centuries, the Rhuys peninsula was covered with salt marshes, which made it prosperous.

The 1914-18 war saw a decline in the salt production of the peninsula. The Lasné marshes converted to oyster-farming and then aqua-culture.

These days, the former salt pans of Lasné, Ludré and Le Passage (about 250 acres altogether) are turning towards nature tourism... for everyone's pleasure.

Tascon island

This island is accessible from the village of Lasné at low tide, and reveals sublime glimpses of the gulf islands: Oeufs (Eggs) island, Oiseaux (Birds) Island, Illur, Illuric and Arz island... without forgetting the peaceful walk (but be careful about the times of the tides!).

Sarzeau

This large commune, famous for its Suscinio château, the favourite residence of the Dukes of Brittany, offers attractive slopes towards the gulf.

Saint-Colombier is the typical example of a dream hamlet for holidays: little *pen-ty* (houses) full of

103

flowers, grouped around the chapel belfry.

After the village of Saint-Colombier, you will arrive at the Duer marshes, now listed as a "great natural site". An observation track will take you to see the many species of birds living off the rich silts of the gulf ("nature" rambles organised all year round).

Just like Saint-Colombier, go on bicycle or on foot to discover the villages of Brillac or Logéo; absolute peace.

Arzon

At the very end of the Rhuys peninsula, Arzon has a very privileged position: on one side, the spray from the Atlantic; on the other, the gentle gulf of Morbihan.

Pen Castel Mill

At the end of the cove formed by Beninze Point (a village with character, to be admired at leisure) and Saint-Nicolas Point, one of the finest mills of the Morbihan stands proudly: the Pen Castel mill.

It was built in the 17th century, and this magnificent tidal mill succeeded the first mill (no doubt built of wood) which belonged to Jean IV de Montfort, Duke of Brittany.

The sluices allow the waters of the gulf to enter, with the incoming tide,

Arzon, its great menhir decorated at the base with an axe, in the village of Le Net en Kermaillard.

and to leave with the ebb tide. The mill thus turned with the tides, as the miller wished, until 1914, when its work was stopped. Take the time to admire its architectural riches: carved dormer windows, chimneys with hoods or caps...

Port-Navalo

The history of this magnificent site is intimately linked with maritime activity.

The Veneti, and then the Romans, understood the value of this natural shelter, well protected from the ocean squalls. In the first century A.D. the famous Greek astronomer and geographer Ptolemy situated it under the name of "Vindana Portus".

During the following centuries, the port developed to become a very active commercial port, so much so that in the middle of the 19th century, eighty schooners and coastal luggers were dedicated to the role of the Port-Navalo customs. Two thousand eight hundred ships put into port here every year!

These days, only the halyards of a few yachts respond to the ocean wind.

 Gulf of Morbihan

MORE INFORMATION?
Tourist office of the pays de Vannes
1, rue Thiers 56000 Vannes
Tel.: 02 97 47 24 34 —
Fax: 02 97 47 29 49
E-mail: office. tourisme. vannes@wanadoo. fr
Two indispensable works: the "Guide to rambling and walking in the Rhuys peninsula". "Vannes and the Morbihan Gulf", collection Routes of Discovery, Pub. Ouest-France.

A well-sheltered cove at the mouth of the Gulf: Port-Navalo.

The tidal mills

The Pen Castel tidal mill is recognised as the jewel of all those still standing in the Morbihan. Most of them were built in the 12th and 13th centuries, and operated according to the same principle, playing with the tides: a waste-weir allowed the pool to be filled by the rising tide. At high tide, the water which had been collected was let out onto the great wheel which could then turn for several hours, allowing the pool to return to its lowest level.

During the spring tides (coefficient greater than 70) the miller and his assistants often worked night and day to take advantage of the two daily tides. During neap tides, they carried out repairs on the mill... or sold fish from the pool. The mills of Mériadec and Pomper (en Baden), very well preserved, worked until the sixties. Apart from these, mill enthusiasts can visit those of Hezo or Berno (Arz island), which are especially interesting.

The Crac'h tidal river mill.

Loire-Atlantique

from the silence of canals to Tuscan lights

THE BRIÈRE REGIONAL NATURE PARK

"This is a land of water, peat and rushes. Savage and secret, it is dotted with islets and criss-crossed by canals. In winter the ducks and the snipe choose it for their winter quarters while the migrating birds find a well-deserved rest here on their long trip.

When the first signs of Spring appear, the iris and the marsh marigolds open up. In the thick fog, over there, a silhouette can be made out: a punt slides into the morning light. Soft music in the waters of the velvety silence of the Brière..."

"The Guérande and Brière Peninsula" Pub. Ouest-France.

*Opposite: **Clisson**,*
the Garenne-Lemot domain.
Detail of the Villa.

The Brière marshes.
Punts waiting for visitors.

Grey heron. *Photo André Mauxion.*

The Brière, a bird paradise

Dozens of species (some them threatened with extinction) come here to find food, to rest and to reproduce, in the "piardes", water meadows and reed beds of the Grand Marais.

• *In the "piardes": in winter: mallards, northern pintails, wigeons, coots... and in spring: black and whiskered terns, thrushes and wagtails...*
• *In the reed beds: in the nesting season, from April to June, there is an abundance of swamp warblers, reed warblers, water rails and the marsh harriers...*
• *In the water meadows: in winter, they welcome migrating birds, (teals and wigeons); and in springtime, ruffs (the only known nesting place in France)...*

To read: "Flora and Fauna of the Brière marshes", a booklet published by the Regional Nature Park.

In these few words, so true and so beautiful, Laurence Vilaine gives a perfect description of the atmosphere of the Brière, the only one of its kind, and the second marshes of France after the Camargue.

It is a real mosaic of canals (the "dredged"), of shallow pools (the "piardes and "copis"), reed beds, water meadows and hillocks. Besides this, and above all, the Brière is the kingdom of birds. The whiskered tern and the Montagu's harrier will welcome you to their little corner of paradise.

Punt trips, in the heart of the marshes

In order to pierce the secrets of the flora, fauna, and the life of the Brière traditions, I placed my confidence in one of the punters licensed to the Regional Nature Park... and never regretted it.

It was at the end of May, hesitating between a timid sun and a turbulent wind, and I "followed the heron" to reach Prises port, the discreet refuge of Hubert Dugué, reputed ornithologist and enthusiastic

Hubert Dugué returning from a trip with several happy visitors.
N.B. Since our reporting, Hubert and his wife have had to leave the Brière despite their willing. In fact, during the summer of the year 2000 several property and hunting fanatics outrageously set fire to their bungalow and their boats. These extremists, convinced of their impunity, finished off their work by burning down the Brière Nature Park house at Saint-Joachim on August 18th. Will the Brière remain a bird paradise for much longer?

storyteller: *"Man fashioned the marshes: the Brière is a vast marsh of 15,000 acres of freshwater, whose level rises or falls according to the rains; in 1988 it was very high (2.6 m) and the Brière looked like a lake because of the abundant rainfall. In 1976 and 1989 it was*

very low (0.6 m), as a result of the sun..."

Hubert understands his marshes from end to end... describing all the details of the flight of the Montagu's harrier and also that of the reed harrier, the wagtail and the hobby falcon...

The punt slides along gently, we have reached the middle of the marshes, a realm of silence and reeds trembling gently to the murmur of the wind... Furtive sentiments of deep peace...

The licensed punters await you at the ports of Bréca, Fedrun and Chausée Neuve.

Ile de Fédrun

This is one of the seven isles in the Saint-Joachim commune and is certainly the most distinctive. A small route goes all around, for walking, between cottages full of flowers and languid punts. Close to the well-known

Brière, the property of its inhabitants

The marsh of the Grande Brière peat bog is the undivided property of its inhabitants. This very special legal status is extremely old, since it was recognised by letters patent from François II, Duke of Brittany, dated August 8th 1461.

Each of the 21 neighbouring communes designates a representative to sit in the syndical Commission of the Grand Brière peatbog, which manages the marsh (the Regional Nature Park can only make suggestions).

One can understand better the origin of the saying: "Briéron, master at home!"

inns, the "Bride's House" is a reminder than in previous days Fédrun was the main manufacturer of wax orange blossoms for the bride's crown (there is a sumptuous exhibition of bridal head-dresses).

In springtime, the marshes deck themselves out with sumptuous bouquets of water irises.

Saint-Malo-de-Guersac: Rozé port and its nature park

Here, there are 62 protected acres with an organised walk of 1.5 km, which is so successful that I would happily call it the marvellous "birds' walk".

The elevated path with ditches on either side winds into the heart of the

At the Rozé nature park, it is possible to learn the art of fishing.

"Piardes " and "copis"

These two words, describing the Grande Brière peat bog, need an explanation.

The "piarde" is a shallow pool, corresponding to former zones where they extracted the peat. They have very precise names: the Eugène "piarde", the Julot "piarde"... When peat was no longer exploited in Brière, the piardes were invaded little by little by the reed beds. This area was reduced significantly, from 2,000 acres in 1945 to 625 acres these days, but it is still a vital site for flora and fauna.
The "copi" is a deeper stretch of water, corresponding to a pool.

pastures and pools, in a loop, leaving from the reception hall. Panels describing the flora and fauna explain the life of the "inhabitants" of the marsh. There are hides for bird-watching, without disturbing them (don't forget your binoculars!).

Saint-André-des-Eaux:
la Chaussée Neuve

This former port, the transit for peat, salt and vegetables, is an excellent observation post these days overlooking the marshes (viewpoint table at the end of the discovery path) and the departure point for punt trips.

Saint-Lyphard

Saint-Lyphard prides itself in being the *"town with 500 cottages"*, scattered around its hamlets with real Breton names: Kerbourg, Kerverne, Kermourand, Kerhinet... Nettles had invaded the ruined walls

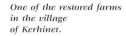

The famous Brière thatched cottages are still built by craftsmen proud of their skill and their architectural heritage.

One of the restored farms in the village of Kerhinet.

of the eighteen houses of the latter, when the Brière Nature Park decided to restore them, at the beginning of the eighties.

Kerhinet village

These days, this former moribund village, is a highlight of the marshes, one of the centres for activities for discovery classes, stopovers, inn, Thatched cottage museum, Artisans House... Kerhinet is alive... and so much the better! Myself, I happily strolled along its flowered alleys, stopping to look at these cottages, which they say belong to former times, but which have benefited from the art of present-day thatchers.

Kerhinet is also the departure point for one of the most beautiful walks in Brière: the thatched cottages and marshes circuit (11 km, marked in yellow).

There are dozens of thatched houses full of flowers scattered around on the way to the village of Kerbourg, which

deserve the claims of the place. According to tradition, the dolmen situated near this hamlet is erected above an underground cave "filled with gold" and is inhabited by small and strange beings, which come out at night. Undoubtedly it was the site of *"human sacrifices"*!

*Herbignac: Ranrouët castle.
At the entrance to the
Grande Brière marshs,
this fortified castle, built
at the beginning of the
13th century by the Assérac
family, is still evidence
of the eminent role it played
over several centuries,
defending the Guérand
peninsula.
With its six imposing and
majestic towers, it gives
a splendid idea of
the evolution of military
architecture, from the 13th to
17th centuries. The powerful
Rochefort and Rieux
families, who succeeded the
Asséracs, had to adapt it to
withstand the progress
of artillery.
The interpretation circuit
and guided visits will reveal
all the secrets of this "castel",
which becomes medieval
again each summer, during
evenings of storytelling and
dancing...*

La Brière

MORE INFORMATION?
Brière Tourist House
*38, rue de la Brière
44410 La Chapelle-des-
Marais
Tel.: 02 40 66 85 01 —
Fax: 02 40 53 91 15*

Brière has the reputation of being a "mysterious land", which is fully justified at the next stop, the Gras bridge, an amazing "Gaul" bridge, with huge slabs of granite thrown across the marsh.

Bréca port

Look carefully at the map of the Grande Brière marsh: Bréca port is exactly opposite to Rozé port, which it joins along a straight canal 9 km long. In 1937 and 1938 the "Northern canal", the "old canal", the "Bréca canal" and the "Rozé canal" were re-engineered to link the banks of the marshes more easily (before this, it was a real labyrinth).

Bréca is very busy in the summer (tours in punts and carts) but rediscovers its charm out of season. All the romance of the Brière is expressed at nightfall, as sung by the poet René Guy Cadou: "*Another evening when I shall go out on the great book of the marshes to write the words of my childhood.*"

The morta

On one of the car-parks of the village of Kerhinet, you will find enormous tree-trunks lying down, which look as though they were burnt. They are the last witnesses of the Brière forest. They sank about six thousand years ago, and were fossilised by vegetal decomposition. The morta was exhumed recently, and attracted sculptors: works by Gérard Desrues, "les landes" in Saint-Lyphard, pipes by Patrice Sébilo in Herbignac.

THE NANTES-BREST CANAL: THE ROYAL WAY THROUGH INLAND BRITTANY

Tourists... and Breton friends, have you walked along the towpath of the Nantes-Brest canal?

The reason I am asking this question is that I am always struck by the contrast between the "crowd" of walkers going along the customs officers' paths following the ocean and the almost deserted canal, whatever the season.

Between Nantes and Brest, you can discover a secret Brittany which I can recommend. Why hesitate? This is a path which is calm and serene, so begin your initiation: between Nantes and Redon, 95 km, after which you will have only one wish: to continue.

Nantes and the Erdre

The adventure begins under the high walls of the castle of the Dukes of Brittany, with the steel frame of lock number 1 Saint-Félix in their shade. This is very popular with "Sunday walkers", with its automatic systems of tele-observation, computer assisted, and is the image of ambient modernism, so let's go on quickly to the Ile de Versailles.

In the heart of the town, this islet is blessed with a fabulous exotic garden with the perfumes of Japan, with its bamboo, cedars and cypresses, sheltering waterfalls and pools, under a wonderland of flowers. Do not forget to visit the Maison de l'Erdre, to understand the secrets of the flora and fauna of this river, the "most beautiful in France" according to Henri IV, king of France and Navarre.

From the Ile de Versailles, turn towards Sucé-sur-Erdre, taking little footpaths (or departmental roads), the cruise boats along the Erdre, or even hiring an electric boat. In this way you will be able to admire the sumptuous dwellings and châteaux on the edge of the banks: la Desnerie, la Poterie, la Gascherie, la Couronnerie, la Buraudière, la Guillaunière...

A royal way... due to an Emperor

In fact, the emperor Napoleon I began building this canal, already imagined by the states of Brittany in preceding centuries.

England, which was master of the seas at the beginning of the 19th century, was against the ambitions of the "Corsican ogre", imposing a blocus on the port of Brest. In order to escape this, the obstacle could be avoided along river-ways as far as Nantes, which was the meaning of the mission entrusted by Bonaparte in 1804 to citizen Bouessel, "structural engineer".

The first works were started in 1806 to finish in ... 1842!

Graulais castle at Blain, the Logis du Roi, (hostelry-restaurant).

The canal at Blain, Surcouf quay.

Sucé-sur-Erdre: the "pearl" of the Erdre

This little commune well deserves its reputation, with its white houses and their flower gardens lost in greenery near the pool. The inhabitants of Nantes often come here in numbers, to walk at weekends. And it is easy to understand why! Here, there is none of the stress of the regional metropolis, just the murmur of sails flapping in the light breeze. At the yacht club, many habitable boats for rental are moored. You can easily reach the Quiheix lock on foot, by bicycle or along the waterway, which is the first artificial section of the canal.

The Isac valley, from Quiheix to Blain

"La Tindière", "la Rabinière"... the locks come one after the other until the Pas d'Heric lock and the Bout-du-Bois mill reach. In 1812, many Spanish prisoners of war were brought near here, to the Jarriais camp. Just as on other of the canal's worksites, they laboured under atrocious conditions... which are difficult to imagine now, along this calm and tranquil towpath.

But now we are reaching Blain, on the Surcouf quay, not bordered by pirate vessels but by welcoming inns, offering the local specialities: sander, pike, and Isac eels, as well as game from the Gâvre forest. After a happy feast, go on to the astonishing Arts and Traditions museum in the town centre (a unique collection of "Twelfth Night santons", boutiques 1900, Christmas cribs) and Groulais castle, the former dwelling of the Clissons and the Rohans. Built in the 12th century, under the orders of Alain IV Fergent Duke of Brittany, it witnessed the fortunes and misfortunes of its successive owners, the sires of Clisson and the powerful seigniors of Rohan.

 The Isac valley

MORE INFORMATION?
Tourist office
Place Jean-Guihard
44130 Blain
Tel.: 02 40 87 15 11 —
Fax: 02 40 79 09 93
Website:
www.cartopole.org

The drawbridge tower (14th century) houses the Fresco Centre, which redecorated the Saint-Roch chapel just as the Romanesque churches were at their origin. This has to be seen!

Another few bends, and here we are in Pont-Miny, under the pink pebble-dash of the Maison du Canal. Take the opportunity to visit the exhibition of the history of the Nantes-Brest canal and discover how the locks work, thanks to sophisticated models. This is also a halt appreciated by ramblers who can spend a comfortable night here.

Before reaching Redon, the cross-roads of Breton canals, don't miss stopping at the Bellion lock, where the little Saint-Jacques chapel recalls the passage of the "jacquets", the Compostelle pilgrims.

In this land where water and earth mingle, the antique city of Durétie used to stand. When and why did it disappear? According to the legend *"Saint Jacques, in person, came up the Vilaine river, and wanted to stop in Rieux. He was chased out under a rain of blows from the washer-women. 'Such an inhospitable town, he cursed, will be destroyed'... and he left straight away to create the city of Redon".*

Fégréac and the Redon marshes

MORE INFORMATION?
Tourist office of Nantes-Atlantique
Place du Commerce
44000 Nantes
Tel.: 02 40 47 04 51
Tourist pays d'accueil of the Three Rivers
Town hall, rue Charles-de-Gaulle, 44130 Blain
Tel.: 02 40 79 16 65 —
Fax: 02 40 79 83 72
To read: "The Nantes-Brest canal"
by Kader Benferhat and Sandra Aubert,
pub. Ouest-France.

Fégréac
and the Redon marshes

Between Blain and Fégréac, the canal flows lazily under the shade of the poplars, oaks and beech, revealing here and there locks full of flowers and wonderful halts... for provisions, such as the charming little port of Guenroët.

Our pleasant journey ends at Saint-Nicolas-de-Redon on the canal towpath of Nantes to... I am convinced, Malestroit, Josselin, Pontivy, Châteaulin which have attracted you... irresistibly!

Fégréac, Saint Jacques statue.

A perfume of Italy, on the banks of the Sèvre.

CLISSON: A MEDIEVAL CITY... WITH A PERFUME OF ITALY

Since 1941, Clisson is no longer Breton.

That year, the Pétain administration under occupation dared kick out of Brittany such a famous stronghold. Shame on them for ever! Did they even know that on the borderlands of the Duchy, Clisson was a feared bastion; or that in the 15th century, François II Duke of Brittany, possessed a fine house in the citadel here.

These days, one can see the two faces of Clisson from the bridge over the Valley (15th century), across the river Sèvre: the medieval side, with its imposing castle erected on the banks of the river, and the "Italian" side with its red roofing tiles, like the Notre-Dame church.

Medieval Clisson

Three buildings bear witness to the grandeur and importance of this city in the Middle Ages.

The castle

Clisson, at the Borderlands of the Duchy of Brittany, held a strategic position over several centuries (from the 11th to the 15th), facing the powerful counties of Anjou and Poitou. Although we have lost trace of the first castle built at the dawn of the year one thousand, on a rocky spur, the stones of

Guillaume de Clisson attacks the Templars

The archives have recorded the bitter fight in the 13th century opposing this seignior of Clisson and the Knights Templar. He was jealous of the rapid growth of their properties, and invaded their domain and ransacked it, carrying off a quantity of riches. Worse still, he killed a man who was a vassal of the Templars, in the Magdeleine cemetery, thus disregarding the right of asylum. The "red monks" claimed justice from Étienne de la Bruère, bishop of Nantes. The latter accepted their plaint, and condemned the impetuous seignior to provide financial compensation and a "freeman called Thébaud le Volant to be given, in perpetuity" in compensation for the murder committed in the cemetery.

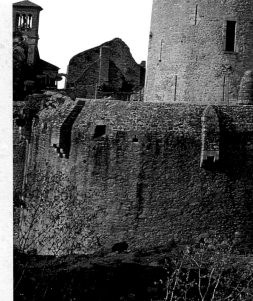

the walls erected in the 13th century by Guillaume, sire of Clisson, are still a reminder of the feudal era.

This seignior, wishing to protect himself from the aggressive intentions of his neighbours, surrounded the town with ramparts and built a fortified castle, whose construction started in 1217, on lands belonging to the "holy mission of the hospital" (the hospital knights of Saint-Jean-de-Jérusalem). During the four following centuries, several bastions and walls strengthened the defences of this citadel.

In 1336, Olivier IV of Clisson was born, future Constable of France. He was companion at arms of the impetuous Bertrand du Guesclin, and wielded his terrible axe on many battlefields.

In the 15th century, François II, Duke of Brittany, transformed the castle into one of his favourite residences and enhanced its military vocation, by building a new enclosure. In the 17th and 18th centuries, his descendants (illegitimate), the Avaugours, continued his work.

The Clisson castle, burned down in 1793 by the Blues (Republican troops) after the French Revolution, during the terrible Vendée wars, was bought in 1962 by the General Council of the Loire-Atlantique department, and has been restored since then.

The Madeleine chapel or the "Knights Templar chapel"

Specialists consider this to be one of the most convincing examples of religious architecture of the Knights Templar: a nave, a choir, an apse, all vaulted under a slightly pointed arch. Just like the facade, it is characterised by its bareness and simplicity, according to the express will of the knights of the Temple.

These famous Knights Templar!

It was a military order, born by and for the crusades, and very early on had an import command post at the gates of the city, which became so wealthy that the fearful sires of Clisson became jealous.

The market halls and Minage Square

These are the last witnesses of the trading activity of the city in the Middle Ages. The "minage" was a tax on cereals and the "maison du minage", where this tax was applied, was built on this square, just next to the castle.

The castle of Clisson is of special interest because it is a site with five hundred years of fortifications. In itself it is a synthesis of French military architecture.

Notre-Dame church, of neo-Romanesque style, is well integrated into its surroundings.

During the 15th century, François II Duke of Brittany often took up residence in Clisson, and decided to cover the old market square. These days, very few medieval market halls still exist, and it is a rare privilege to admire the timberwork (oak and chestnut) and the linking of the beams at that time. A final detail, this hall "miraculously" escaped the destruction of the Vendée wars, for the simple reason that it was used as a camp for both sides, the Blues and the Whites.

Clisson, "the Italian"

Clisson was economically ruined by the Vendée wars, but recovered at the beginning of the 19th century, under a Tuscan perfume which suits it so well: Roman roof tiles, arcades, gemel windows, villas and maritime pines...

But where did this new landscape come from?

Three artists, in love with Italy, introduced this new architecture to Clisson and its valley: the Cacault brothers and François-Frédéric Lemot. Pierre and François Cacault (originally from Nantes) had been chased out of Italy by the anti-Republican uprisings and returned to France to settle in Clisson in 1798. Lemot, a well-known Parisian sculptor and friend of François, joined them soon after.

All three saw in Clisson the French equivalent of the Roman countryside painted by Nicolas Poussin (1594-1665) and Claude Lorrain (1600-1680).

Channelled roof tiles, thin bricks, and semicircular arches were used to decorate the newly built dwellings, and also the mills, tanneries and factories on the banks of the river.

Lemot, who bought the Garenne woods in 1805, built the Maison du Jardinier here between 1811 and 1815, in the same Italian style, which soon became known as the "Clisson style". It was the first "Italian" villa which was to inspire many others, as you can see by strolling through the narrow streets of the town.

There are three buildings, in particular, which seem to me to exhale perfectly this perfume of Italy.

Notre-Dame church

It was built between 1887 and 1889, and has no resemblance to the "neo-Gothic" churches in fashion at that time. It is greatly inspired by the old

Roman Basilica, with its large rectangular hall divided into three naves.

The Garenne-Valentin Italian-style villa

Built on the remains of the old Benedictine convent of the Trinity, the Garenne-Valentin needed twenty years of work (1810-1830) and unfortu-

Detail from the Villa-Lemot.

nately was disfigured in 1902.

However, with its park designed by the landscape gardener Lechappé, it is an example of the ideal "villa à l'italienne" designed by Lemot.

The Garenne-Lemot domain, at Gétigné-Clisson

Located 3 km away from Clisson, this is the most successful example of the "Italian dream" pursued by Lemot and so well expressed in its three forms:

The park

This is composed like the landscape of a classical painting; presenting nature over 30 acres criss-crossed by paths, revealing here and there statues inspired by Antiquity, monuments such as the "Temple of Friendship" and even... a grotto dedicated to Héloïse!

The Gardener's House

Designed by Mathurin Crucy, with its tiled roofs and decorative patterns in bricks, its high pigeon tower and its yard surrounded by a crenellated wall, it recalls the fortified farms of Tuscany.

The Villa Lemot

Construction began in 1824, on the model of the Patrician estates of Rome: colonnades in semicircle, loggia, porch, pediment and gazebo.

The arcades of the Gardener's House.

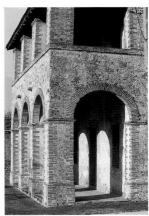

The gardener's house of the Garenne-Lemot domain: there are very interesting exhibitions all year round. Property of the Loire-Atlantique General Council.

 The Garenne Lemot domain

MORE INFORMATION?
La Garenne-Lemot
44190 Gétigné
Tel.: 02 40 54 75 85 —
Fax 02 40 03 99 22
Website: http ://www.
cg44.fr/special/GL
Tourist office
Place du Minage, BP 9124,
44191 Clisson Cedex
Tel.: 02 40 54 02 95 —
Fax 02 40 54 07 77
E-mail: ong-clisson. com

Useful addresses for touring in Brittany

Fédération régionale des pays d'accueil touristiques de Bretagne (Regional Federation of the tourist pays d'accueil of Brittany)
BP 24 — 56301 Pontivy Cedex. Tel.: 02.97.51.46. 16 — Fax: 02.97.51.42.40

Comités départementaux de tourisme (Departmental Committees for tourism)
Côtes-d'Armor
29, rue des Promenades — BP 4620 — 22046 Saint-Brieuc Cedex 2. Tel.: 02.96.62.72.00
Finistère
11, rue Théodore-Le Hars — 29104 Quimper. Tel.: 02.98.76.20.70
Ille-et-Vilaine
4, rue Jean-Jaurès — 35000 Rennes. Tel.: 02.99.78.47.47
Morbihan
PIBS — 56009 Vannes. Tel.: 02.97.54.06.56
Loire-Atlantique
2, allée Baco — BP 20502 — 44005 Nantes Cedex. Tel.: 02.51.72.95.30

Comité régional du tourisme de Bretagne (Regional Committee for tourism in Brittany)
1, rue Raoul-Ponchon — 35069 Rennes Cedex. Tel.: 02.99.36.15.15 — Fax: 02.99.28.44.40 — Minitel: 3615 BRETAGNE

Union bretonne du tourisme rural (Breton Union for rural tourism)
111, bld De-Lattre-de-Tassigny — CS 74223 — 35042 Rennes Cedex. Tel.: 02.99.59.43.33

Accueil paysan (Peasant welcome)
3, square Ludovic-Travieux — 35000 Rennes. Tel.: 02.99.86.01.01

Randobalad
8, rue du Louis-d'Or — 35000 Rennes. Tel.: 02.99.30.89.11

Rando Breizh
1, rue Raoul-Ponchon — 35069 Rennes Cedex

Maison de la Bretagne (Brittany House)
203, bld Saint-Germain 75007 Paris. Tel.: 01.53.63.11.50 — Fax: 01.53.63.11.57
Internet: http//www. brittanytourism. com — Internet région : http//www. region-bretagne. fr
E-mail: tourism@region-bretagne. fr

Ligue pour la Protection des Oiseaux (LPO)
Station ornithologique de l'Ile-Grande 22560 Pleumeur-Bodou. Tél. 02 96 91 91 40

SEPNB Bretagne Vivante
186, rue Anatole-France 29200 Brest. Tél. 02 98 49 07 18

Old oyster beds in the Etel river, oppposite Saint-Cado island.
Property of the Belz commune (Morbihan).

CONTENTS

Finistère, a land of character 47

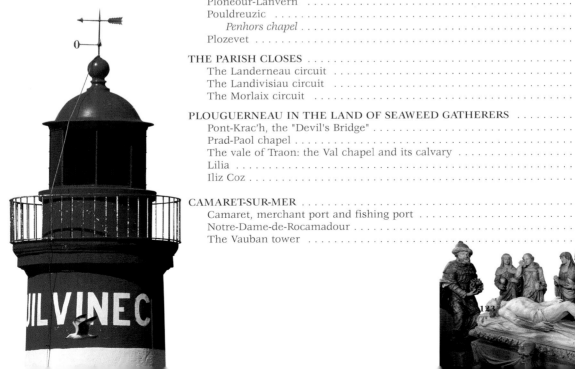

Ile de Bréhat, Paon Point.

Graphic Design: Terre de Brume
Cartography: Patrick Mérienne

© 2001 - Édilarge S.A., Éditions Ouest-France
Cet ouvrage a été achevé d'imprimer par l'imprimerie Pollina à Luçon (85)
COMPUTER TO PLATE
I.SB.N. 2.7373.2831.4 - N° d'éditeur : 4207.01.06.04.01
Dépôt légal : avril 2001

"For the chosen few, visiting Brittany is not what counts. What counts is to leave it while wishing to stay and live there, the ear glued against this deep murmuring shell. And its appeal is that of a cloister whose wall has a breach open to the high seas: the sea, the wind, the sky, the bare earth, and nothing. This is the realm of the soul."

Julien Gracq

Summit of Menez-Hom
the Crozon peninsula
(Finistère).